New
Voices
Playwrights
Theatre

Annual Anthology
of Short Plays
2021

Edited by

John Bolen

New Voices Playwrights Theatre
a 501(c)(3) corporation

P.O. Box 53921, Irvine, CA 92619-3921
newvoicesplaywrights.org
newvoicesplaywrights@gmail.com

Table of Contents

Foreword

Theatres looked forward to reopening this autumn with the tools, that is the vaccines, ready to put COVID-19 in the past. However it seems that a new pandemic, that is the pandemic of the unvaccinated, is threatening with a far more virulent strain in the Delta Variant. There is frustration for the vaccinated populace to face a possible return to closures and other measures to fight this oncoming menace, a menace created by multiple reasons ranging from fear of the vaccines' side-effects to misinformation campaigns that have alarmed the unvaccinated.

After the pandemic of the Spanish Flu in 1918, as reported by Charlotte M. Canning in *American Theatre* magazine, "major literary figures of the 1920s and after ignored the flu in their work, and offered audiences no representations of the disease that rivaled the Great War (WWI) in its body count." Some of our playwrights have tackled the inconvenience of this current outbreak in their plays included here; but they have not tackled the other reasons that have created this situation of a new sudden increase of hospitalizations and deaths.

So plays written for Zoom presentations will continue for the time being with their own set of rules limiting any physical motion. "Talking heads" as playwrights refer to these plays may continue to be the norm for a while longer. Despite this, theatres are planning to open, going into rehearsals for full productions. All are hoping for the best.

It will be interesting to see if the playwriting community creates plays that deal with the horror of so many dead and the reasons for those deaths. Perhaps with time, it will be easier to grasp why hesitancy and fear in the populace of the unvaccinated would lead to so much disease and death.

Watch for the **New Voices Holiday Plays 2021**, the next in our series, available in October.

John Bolen, Editor
Vice President
New Voices Playwrights Theatre

The Beatles Said It All

By

John Bolen

John Bolen is a novelist/playwright/actor living in Southern California. He has been published by *Applause Theatre & Cinema Books* three times *(Hal Leonard Publishing), Independentplay(w)rights, Indigo Rising, Scars Publications, The Write Place at the Write Time, OC180news, Eunoia Review* and *YouthPLAYS*. John's plays have been produced in theatres throughout the U.S. including: New Jersey Repertory; STAGEStheatre, CA; Chance Theater, CA; Cabrillo Playhouse, CA; Theatre@First, MA; NewGate Theatre, RI; Newport Theatre Arts Center, CA; Thalian Hall Studio Center, NC; Costa Mesa Playhouse, CA; Secret Rose Theatre, CA; The Asylum Theatre, CA; Lincoln Square Theatre, Chicago, IL; Malibu Stage Company, CA; Vanguard Theatre Ensemble, CA; Garden Grove Playhouse, CA; Red Room Theatre, NYC; Gallery Theatre, CA; Stage Door Repertory Theatre, CA; and the Empire Theatre, CA. His short story collection ***Nothing for Christmas & Other Holiday Tales*** and his novel ***Aurelia's Magic*** are available on Amazon. As an actor, John has worked on stage, in film and TV, and has recorded 35 books on CD. John is the Vice-President of the New Voices Playwrights Theatre & Workshop.

CHARACTERS

George, male, 55-65

Ida, female, 55-65

Bigelow, male, 35

> *The setting is a storage space in one of those large storage facilities. George and Ida stand looking at the piles of boxes. NOTE: the underlined texts are lyrics to be sung. Actors should learn the melody that corresponds to the specific lyric.*

George: *(Pointing first right then left.)* You take the high road and I'll take the low road.

Ida: Anonymous doesn't work.

George: I wasn't playing, Ida, but we can play if you like.

Ida: You go first.

George: **(Bohemian Rhapsody/Queen.)** <u>Mama, I've killed a man; put a gun against his head, pulled my trigger now he's dead.</u>

> *They begin looking through the boxes*

Ida: What a Mercurial start, George.

George: Funny

Ida: **(Everybody Loves a Clown/ Gary Lewis & the Playboys.)** <u>Everybody loves a clown, so why don't you? Everybody laughs at the things I say and do.</u>

George: Gary Lewis of Gary Lewis and the Playboys, Leon Russell and... Snuff Garrett? I see Scaramouch the Clown is the thread. You always surprise me, Ida. *Everybody Loves a Clown* was written a decade before we were born.

Ida: You're the one that surprises me, George. I've been saving that for years waiting for a clown reference and you just rattle off Snuff Garrett.

George: There was hesitation.

Ida: It's your go again, smart ass.

George: This box that I'm looking at seems to be stuff from your parents; photo albums and such. I'll put it in your pile. Let's see... **(Gary, Indiana/The Music Man.)** Gary, Indiana; Gary , Indiana; Gary, Indiana, my home sweet home.

Ida: That's from *The Music Man*. Meredith Wilson. This box is filled with fishing stuff.

George: I wondered where that went. Who put that in storage?

Ida: I suspect one of the kids when we did that great purge of the garage. We still couldn't get enough room to park a car. I wonder how many people actually park their cars in their garages.

George: People who have owned their houses for less than five years, probably. Just put the box in my pile.

Ida: **(Back Home Again in Indiana/American classic.)** Back home again, in Indiana, and it seems that I can see, the gleaming candlelight still shining bright.

George: Are we really doing songs over a century old?

Ida: This could be the last time we play; let's make it the Master's Edition.

George: James Hanley.

Ida: He wrote the music, but Ballard MacDonald did the lyrics. That's a point for me.

George: Impressive! You've really been saving up, haven't you? This box seems to be filled with dresses.

Bigelow enters unseen by Ida.

Ida: That will have my wedding dress in there. Save that in my pile, G.O.

Bigelow: Do you really need to save that?

Ida turns, surprised.

Ida: Why did you come in, Big? I asked you not to.

Bigelow: Maybe I can help in figuring out what to keep. Do you really need a keepsake from a failed marriage?

Ida: I have a daughter that might want that dress whose memories might not be of a failed marriage. She would rightly have remembrance of good times.

George: Definitely rightly. Who is this?

Ida: Sorry, I asked him not to come in, G.O. This is Bigelow Johnson.

Bigelow: G.O. Is that short for Giovanni?

Ida: They're his first and middle initials. George Orwell Penman is the total name. His parents had high hopes.

Bigelow: So few people meet their parents' expectations.

Ida: You're being rude, Big. Big's middle name is his mother's family name, Long.

George: Big Long Johnson. Well, you must be very proud if you met your parents' expectations.

Bigelow: It's Bigelow.

George: Of course it is. Did Ida tell you her given birth name? It's Ida Lovett Hardigan. You two make quite a match.

Ida: He's screwing with you, Big. My middle name is Louise. Now go back out. I told you that you shouldn't come in.

Bigelow: I can help carrying out the good stuff and the trash.

George: Trash? You feel you have some right to call our keepsakes trash? Why don't you stand in the corner over there, boy toy, until you're needed? Wait, you're really too old to be a boy toy.

Bigelow: I'm not a toy, and I'll stand where I damn well...

Ida: Stand in the corner, out of the way, Big. There is a ton of stuff I have to go through. *(To George.)* This box is all the kids' drawings and crafts that used to hang on the refrigerator. I'd like it...

George: Can we split it?

Bigelow: Where do you intend to put that, Ida?

Ida: In the garage.

Bigelow: We won't have room for the car if you put a bunch of stuff...

George: A lot faster than five years. It's my turn, right? **(A House is Not a Home/Bacharach-David.)** <u>A chair is still a chair, even when there's no one sitting there. But a chair is not a house and a house is not a home when there's no one there to hold you tight, and no one there you can kiss goodnight.</u>

Ida: Hal David; music by Burt Bacharach. Let's not do sad songs.

George: I thought this was the Master's Edition. How can you do the Master's Edition if you don't use sad songs?

Bigelow: Is this that stupid trivia game you were talking about, Ida?

George: I take offense at that, too-old-to-be-a-boy-toy. This game is way beyond trivial. **(Come Out and Play/Offspring.)** <u>Hey man, you disrespecting me? Take him out.</u>

Ida: **(Come Out and Play/Offspring.)** *(Using a bad Mexican accent.)* <u>You got to keep them separated.</u>

   Both George and Ida break out laughing.

George: **(Come Out and Play/Offspring.)** <u>Hey, they don't pay no mind, if you under 18... Er, 35... you won't be doing any time.</u> *(Making a sinister motion towards Bigelow.)* <u>Hey, come out and play.</u>

Bigelow: Are you really calling me out, you old fart?

Ida: Dexter Holland of the Offspring. And Big, G.O. and I are the exact same age.

George: Ooooh, who you calling old? You stepped in it there, not-quite-boy-toy. No hanky-panky tonight.

Bigelow: You just keep pushing it, Jack-ass.

George: Okay, I will.

Ida: Guys, will you please tone down the testosterone?

George: This box has baby shoes, silver baby cups; all that kind of stuff. I want this one.

Ida: I don't think so. It's mine by right.

George: How do you figure that?

Ida: I'm the mother.

George: So, I'm the father.

Ida: You know in any court of law...

George: I thought we weren't doing that.

Bigelow: I thought you and I, Ida, were starting something all brand new. Why do you need these remembrances from the past?

Ida: If you don't have something intelligent to say, why don't you just not say it?

George: Damn Right! Just take your Long Johnson back to the corner. We'll put this box in the "We're going to fight about later" pile.

Ida: Fine. The bridge of *A House Is Not a Home* goes <u>Now and then, I call your name</u> so (**I Call Your**

Name/Beatles.) <u>I call your name, but you're not there.</u>
<u>Was I to blame, for being unfair?</u>

George: Lennon-McCartney, but mostly John Lennon.

Bigelow: How can you keep on playing this stupid
game?

Ida: It's not stupid. And it keeps us from tearing each
other apart.

George: It's how we met, if you must know.

Bigelow: What? You didn't tell me this, Ida.

George: It's true. Ida was in a bar back in our college
years. It was her first time in a bar, using her brand new
fake I.D. Her roommate was in a lip-lock with some
guy on the dance floor, so I approached her and lacking
any smooth lines, posed the question of who wrote the
song playing on the jukebox.

Ida: A lot of fractured fairy tales there. My roommate
and I had often come to that bar, because if you were
even a half decent-looking female, the bartender never
carded you. And when G.O. came up to me, he was all
tongue-tied, so I asked him to name who wrote the
song; and over twenty-five years of the game
commenced.

George: **(Two of Us/Beatles.)** <u>You and I have</u>
<u>memories, longer than the road that stretches out ahead.</u>

Ida: Lennon-McCartney's *Two of Us*; but this was
written all by Paul.

Bigelow: Grab your purse, Ida. We're leaving.

Ida: But I...

Bigelow: No buts; I'm telling you we're going.

Ida: Telling me?

Bigelow: Everything around this man is toxic. We have a brand new story to write; we don't need games from the past.

Ida: Telling me?

Bigelow: Goddamnit! Grab you purse and let's get out of here.

> *In Bigelow's frustration, he kicks the box holding the baby shoes and cups across the room, things from inside pouring out onto the floor.*

Ida: *(Shrieking.)* Aaaaaaah!!! My baby things!!!

> *Like a banshee, Ida races at Bigelow and punches him in the face. When he steps back stunned, she kicks him squarely in the crotch. Bigelow falls to his knees, gasping for breath.*

George: Wow! Right in the Long Johnson; although even worse, right in the Long Johnson *accoutrements (Using the French pronunciation.)*. That hurt me just to watch. Breathe slower, Bigelow, or you'll hyperventilate. Here, let me help you.

> *George helps Bigelow to his feet, then grabbing him by the scruff of the neck, suddenly runs him off the stage.*

Bigelow: *(Off stage.)* Owwww!

> *George and Ida pick up the baby shoes and cups, putting them back in the box.*

George: **(Norwegian Wood/Beatles.)** <u>I once had a girl, or should I say she once had me.</u>

Ida: *Norwegian Wood.* This was John Lennon this time.

George: What a pair we make.

George and Ida sit on a box, hand in hand.

Ida: What am I going to do?

George: **(If I Fell/Beatles.)** <u>'Cause I've been in love before, and I've found that love is more than just holding hands.</u> The Beatles really said it all.

Ida: I want to go home.

George: *(Disappointed.)* Oh.

Ida: Our home.

George: *(Happy now.)* Oh!

George stands and offers Ida his arm. She takes it, stands, and for a moment they look into each other's eyes.

George & Ida: **(Tow Of Us/Beatles.)** *(Singing together.)* <u>On our way back home; bum bum-bum, we're on our way home; bum bum-bum, we're on our way home; bum bum-bum, we're going home.</u>

As George and Ida sing the last words, they are exiting the stage.

<u>End of play.</u>

Entangled

By

Michael Buss

Michael Buss is a playwright/actor/software developer and lives in Santa Ana, Southern California. He was the second President of New Voices Playwrights Theatre, of which he is a founder member. Being originally English, a sly, Pythonesque edge often creeps into his text.

Eleven of Michael's holiday plays have been published under the title "Seasonings," and are available for your enjoyment or performance from Amazon.com. https://www.amazon.com/dp/1734945001

Michael Buss's short plays have nearly all been produced in Southern California: The Theatre District, CA; Chance Theater, CA; STAGEStheatre, CA; Vanguard Theatre Ensemble, CA; Cabrillo Playhouse, CA; Costa Mesa Playhouse, CA; Stage Door Repertory Theatre, CA; The Gallery Theatre, CA; Empire Theatre, CA; Newport Theatre Arts Center, CA. He has also had full length workshop productions at South Coast Repertory, STAGEStheatre, and Stage Door Repertory Theatre.

Readers wishing to see more of Michael's plays may visit http://mbuss.com/plays.php

CHARACTERS

Joss, male, 30s, a writer.

Hannah, female, 30s, a physicist.

> *The summer of 2021; COVID is in retreat.. The settings are an office, a supermarket, a restaurant, and a park. These are all indicated by minimal set pieces on various parts of the stage. Note, although the script indicates scenes, they flow almost seamlessly from one to the next.*
>
> *SCENE 1: We are in an office. On stage left are a small desk, laptop and a phone. Joss stands and breaks the fourth wall.*

Joss: I'm a journalist, with a regular column in a monthly science magazine. Probably too absorbed trying to keep up with the latest news from research labs around the world to form any attachments. Like everyone else I still have to remain grounded. This particular day I was at the supermarket.

> *SCENE 2: In a supermarket he dons his mask. Lights change to indicate the change of scene. Upstage, center. A shelf unit holds a selection of cereals. Joss has his hands full with too many grocery items.*

Joss: Dammit. I knew I should've grabbed a basket.

> *He picks a packet of grits from the shelf and uses his chin to stabilize his provisions. Hannah enters, right, also wearing a mask, squeezes past Joss: in the aisle and accidentally bumps*

> *into his arm. He drops all his groceries! She drops her basket and her few groceries spill out. They are equally alarmed.*

I'm so sorry, I didn't see you.

Hannah: *(Flustered.)* Oh my God. I'm so clumsy. I just wasn't looking. That was entirely my fault.

> *They gaze at the floor for a second then both stoop down to start picking up.*

Joss: Huh! Looks like you buy the same stuff I buy.

Hannah: Yah; for busy people always on the go.

Joss: No time for gourmet cooking.

Hannah: You said it. Look, I'm sorry. I know I just said that, but I'm already late for an appointment. Bye!

> *She grabs Joss's box of grits, tosses it in her basket, and just before her exit, loudly mutters to the audience,*

Asshole!

Joss: *(Looking at what's left, trying to hold his stuff more effectively.)* And to cap it all she took my grits. *(Calling out.)* Hey; hey lady. You got...

> *But she's gone! Joss helplessly holds out a box of raisins and cinnamon spiced oatmeal.*

You got beautiful eyes!

> *Lights dim briefly.*

> *SCENE3:In a restaurant represented by a small
> table and two chairs, stage right. There is a
> stand-up menu, salt and pepper. Joss sits, takes
> the menu. His mask is on the table.*

Joss: Last thing I wanted for breakfast was oatmeal
with raisins! Anyway, I already had an appointment
with the head of a secret government physics facility
doing research into quantum entanglement. Since I
didn't have clearance to enter the lab itself, we had
arranged to meet over appetizers. *(Pause.)* Now I know
what you're thinking, but at the time I had no idea.

> *Joss resumes his examination of the menu and
> sets up his iPad. Hannah enters the restaurant,
> looking around, uncertain whom she should be
> meeting. Removing her mask, she approaches
> Joss.*

Hannah: Excuse me, but are you the journalist I'm
supposed... *(Her voice tails off.)*

Joss: *(Jumping up.)* Yes, absolutely! I mean, probably,
since there's no-one else here.

Hannah: Great. I'm Doctor Hannah Hansen. You spoke
with my secretary earlier.

Joss: Just to confirm, yes. *(Extends a hand, then
awkwardly drops it.)* I keep forgetting; CDC rules, and
all that.

Hannah: So you must be...

Joss: *(A little nervous.)* Joss. That's right. Joss Waters.
The journalist.

Hannah: *(Slightly teasing.)* Ah, *the* journalist! The anti-typical precursor of all journalists. How very reassuring. I wouldn't want to be interviewed by just *any* old journalist.

Joss: *(Tactfully ignoring the jest.)* Doctor Hansen, it's very good to meet you. I've long been an admirer of your work. Please, let's sit. More comfortable.

They settle into their chairs.

Hannah: I'd be more comfortable if you called me Hannah. Only my interns call me Doctor.

Joss: Hah! I don't think they, the academic establishment, that is, award doctorates for journalism.

Hannah: And you would be wrong! You can get a PhD. in journalism at, I think, Columbia Journalism School.

Joss: You knew that?

Hannah: Only because I looked you up last night to see what sort of person was presuming to write an article about me.

Joss: Isn't that a bit...

Hannah: Intrusive? Excessive? I don't think so. After all you've done background on me also. Did you think that improper?

Joss: No, not in the least.

Hannah: So I read that at one time you toyed with the idea of a more academic life rather than mixing it with oddballs and weirdoes just to make a living.

Joss: Well, as sure as polar bears don't hunt elephants, I don't think you are a...

Hannah: A weirdo?

Joss: No. But you do work with weird stuff at the lab.

Hannah: And that is so true. May I borrow the menu?

Joss: *(Handing over the menu.)* Sure! Oh... and whatever you have, it's on me.

Hannah: Thanks. At least you have paid employment. I am at the mercy of whomsoever I can persuade to stump up cash for the next stage of my research. Good job I don't have to support a family.

> *Hannah holds the menu in front of her face. Joss can only see her eyes.*

Joss: Now this IS weird.

Hannah: What is?

Joss: You, holding the menu like that.

Hannah: And why shouldn't I?

Joss: No, of course, you can. But... your eyes. Only your eyes. They seem familiar-like...

Hannah: Are you a psychic when you're not a journalist?

Joss: Here, let me show you.

> *He takes the menu form Hannah and holds it up to his face, watching her.*

Hannah: *(Slowly.)* Oh my God!

Joss: You get it?

Hannah: *(It's coming back.)* I was in the supermarket, shopping.

Joss: In a hurry, I think.

Hannah: I bumped into you... with a mask on.

Joss: Both of us.

Hannah: Your stuff, it went everywhere.

Joss: So I'm not psychic. That was you!

Hannah: I'm so sorry.

Joss: Did you know you took my grits?

Hannah: I found out when I got home, putting the things away.

Joss: They would have been my breakfast; with a coupla links of sausage. But oatmeal with raisins?

Hannah: *(Softly.)* You don't like them, do you?

Joss: No.

Hannah: And I don't like grits.

Joss: After you'd left the aisle, I did wonder if I heard you say something. Like a Parthian shot. Good word, that. Parthian.

Hannah: *(Buries her head in her hands for a moment.)* Yes, I know what a Parthian shot is. You must think I am the most awful person you could have hoped to meet today. I have no excuse. Wait, I do. I was just overwrought with frustrations at work, and panicking about a meeting I was due to chair within the hour.

Joss: I'll tell you what I thought; if I dare.

Hannah: Dare?

Joss: Yes, I saw so little of you in that brief moment. But when you'd gone I thought, *what beautiful eyes!* Then you were gone forever. But now, now we meet again... (*A beat.*) can I have my grits back?

Hannah: (*Bursts out laughing.*) Oh, you silly man! Of course you can. But I insist on a fair trade.

Joss: (*Nodding.*) Your oatmeal and raisins.

Hannah: (*Getting serious.*) Look, I don't have all day. We need to get some work done.

Joss: I'll order. Hey, waiter, you have a moment? Oh good.

> *He holds up the menu for the imaginary waiter to see. He points at the menu items.*

I'll have THIS, and the lady will have this one. (*A pause.*) Yes, with raisins.

Hannah: Y'know. I'm getting to like you.

Joss: (*To Hannah.*) Coffee all right with you? (*She nods her head. Then to the waiter.*) Yeah, two coffees. (*Back to Hannah.*) OK. We'll skip all the background stuff for now; though I will have to check what I've researched to see if it's accurate. What I really want to get into is entanglement.

Hannah: I thought we were getting down to work?

Joss: *(Protesting.)* No. That's not what I meant. I was referring...

Hannah: I know what you meant, Joss. I'm teasing. Quantum particle entanglement.

Joss: Exactly.

Hannah: You want me to explain it?

Joss: Well, I have a pretty good idea. But I heard that you were breaking new ground and experimenting to see whether entanglement works at the <u>macro</u> level.

Hannah: Whoa! Hold up there, cowboy! Let's see if we can walk before we can run. You really know what quantum entanglement is?

Joss: *(Cautiously.)* I think so.

Hannah: All right. If you wrap this round your neck, you've come to the right place.

Joss: If I get entangled?

Hannah: *(Laughing.)* Yes! Go on tell me.

Joss: Well, I don't understand the math.

Hannah: Hardly anybody does. But I do. So go on. This could be interesting.

Joss: *(Taking a deep breath.)* So, the inner world of what happens inside atoms, of how electrons, protons and neutrons relate, is called quantum mechanics. And it gets deeper, because those particles, if I can call them that, actually break down into even smaller and very strange particles; gluons, muons, baryons, Higgs bosons, and the like, that you physicists create in your particle accelerators.

Hannah: Well, that's a good junior high beginning. So what about entanglement?

Joss: Einstein called it "spooky action at a distance."

Hannah: You got that right.

Joss: Well, if you split one of the larger particles, like an electron, the two bits may fly off in different directions, but somehow they remain connected. As though they both know what the other is doing.

Hannah: Like spin?

Joss: This is where I'm on thin ice.

Hannah: I'll tell you; plain man's version, mind you.

Joss: I'd be glad of that.

Hannah: These very minute particles have a number of properties... not houses in Santa Barbara... but qualities or behaviors that we call properties. One of them is spin; another, angular momentum, and location. But let's just take spin.

Joss: *(Setting his mobile phone on the table.)* Can I record this?

Hannah: Well, yeah, but it's pretty elementary.

Joss: Hah. Elementary! I like the pun.

Hannah: It's a very old pun.

Joss: Sorry.

> *As Hannah explains she gesticulates*
> *expansively to help conceptualize what we*
> *cannot see.*

Hannah: When we say *spin* we don't mean the particle is actually spinning, like a ball. It's just a word, really, so that we can say when one particle's spin direction is UP, the other particle's spin is always DOWN. And if one particle reverses spin, so does the other, instantly. And it doesn't matter how far apart they are; just a few millimeters, or half way across the universe. It's as though they are always connected by a magical telephone wire so that whatever one is doing the other does the opposite. And this drove Einstein mad; the information about what each particle is doing travels faster than light!

Joss: Faster than light! How is that even possible?

Hannah: We don't know. We just know that the particles are entangled and always keep in touch.

Joss: *(Getting it.)* Big question, now. What happens when they meet up again, these particles, if that ever could happen?

Hannah: *(Still gesticulating.)* Well, let's assume that the original electron, or whatever, is in a zero state. Then when it splits the two sub-particles have to obey the laws of the universe about conserving energy, and so on. But they are now busily doing their own thing; but always the opposite of each other. Spin up; spin down. So when they meet up again they cancel each other out and return to the original zero state. Energy has been conserved. And that's the end of the spooky action at a distance, the entanglement.

Joss: This is mind blowing.

Hannah: Yes; you're a writer. Now you try explaining that in a play. You do write plays, don't you? Most writers do at some point, I'm told.

Joss: *(Hesitating.)*Ye-es. If I wanted to put the audience to sleep.

Hannah: *(Laughing.)* All right. Enough for now.

Joss: Hang on, I have one more question.

Hannah: Only one?

Joss: Just one... for now, until I give you back your oatmeal.

Hannah: And you get your grits*! (Chuckles.)*. But go ahead, anyway.

Joss: Right. It's this business of macro-entanglement. You know, with things bigger than sub-atomic particles.

Hannah: Made of lots of atoms or molecules?

Joss: I think so.

Hannah: I am working on this right now. I have experiments running even as we speak, back at the lab. There so small you can't see them with the naked eye.

Joss: I mean, can whole organisms get entangled? Like two pieces of chocolate, or... to illustrate... something that happened in my kitchen last week.

Hannah: This sounds highly improbable.

Joss: No, no. Hear me out. Even if you laugh at me.

Hannah: Go on.

Joss: Well I use packets of Stevia to sweeten my coffee, or tea. I neatly slice round the top of the box in which they are sold, than pull out a small packet each time I grab the coffee. Instant coffee, I'm afraid. There are always spare boxes of Stevia in the pantry.

Hannah: And this is about macro entanglement? Sure it's not *macaroni* entanglement.

Joss: No! Stevia. So I was getting low on the little packets. Then by the back door I see another box of Stevia - empty. The top torn off. And in an instant, faster than the speed of light, I know the state of the box of Stevia next to the coffee crystals.

Hannah: And?

Joss: I knew it was full. In the opposite state from the empty one.

Hannah: And how was that possible if you did not previously know.

Joss: This is it! I have a room-mate who took it upon himself to replenish the supply. But I didn't know.

Hannah: And that's entanglement?

Joss: Well the information traveled pretty fast to me, the observer. Two opposite states, one box empty, one box full, and all that.

Hannah: *(Chuckling again.)* Joss, I suspect you're winding me up. And I might just take the bait.

Joss: Whatever that means. So, do you thing human beings can get entangled?

Hannah: Oh yes, but not with the meaning we use as physicists.

Joss: Physicists never get entangled?

Hannah: Nope! Emotional imagination!

> *The lights briefly dim, come up again, to indicate the passage of time.*

> *SCENE 4: In the park, Josh stands one side anxiously shifting his weight from one foot to the other.*

Joss: Will she show up? I mean, it's a nice park. I like the way the sun dapples through the leaves in the late afternoon. We texted this morning so I know she'll be free by now. The weekend is about to begin! My guess is we'll probably feed the ducks. See, I got bread!

> *Hannah appears, opposite. Joss sees her and they converge somewhere in the middle of the setting.*

Hannah: Sorry I'm a bit late.

Joss: No, you're fine. It's a lovely afternoon to wait for someone with pretty eyes.

Hannah: Now watch it. I'm a physicist!

Joss: And I'm a journalist. A fact-based, investigative journalist who sometimes writes plays.

Hannah: Pax!

Joss: Huh! No-one's said that to me since I took Latin at school.

> *Hannah daringly links arms with Joss and they begin to stroll slowly.*

I got bread for the ducks.

Hannah: Bread is not really good for ducks. Did you mom never tell you?

Joss: She died when I was 13. My dad brought me up.

Hannah: I'm sad to hear that.

Joss: I'll bring worms next time.

Hannah: Did you finish the article?

Joss: Yes, I was up pretty late. But I hit the deadline. Trouble is, I don't know what my dyspeptic editor will do with it. "Oh," he'll probably say, "too much science. People don't want science. They don't understand it, and they won't put in the effort to try."

Hannah: But you do. <u>And</u> you got vaccinated!

Joss: Because I follow the science!

Hannah: Stop being so topical. You sound like a commercial. I have something far more important to share with you.

Joss: Oh, do tell!

Hannah: Your so-called psychic recollections got me thinking. You see we are just about the same age.

Joss: So?

Hannah: When I told you I grew up in Bend, Oregon, you were strangely silent.

Joss: I didn't like Bend.

Hannah: Me neither. But when you're a kid you don't make the decisions. And on an inkling I went though some of my old school yearbooks.

Joss: Self-inflicted punishment! Now you are going to shock me.

Hannah: Yes, I found you! We were both eleven. At the same school.

Joss: *(Very quietly.)* I know.

Hannah: You knew? Why didn't you say?

Joss: Because I made a fool of myself and I hoped it would remain forgotten forever.

Hannah: Why, whatever did you do? Tell me. I know you won an essay competition. See, the brilliance showed even back then. So what did you do?

Joss: You don't remember?

Hannah: I'd tell you if I did.

Joss: I wrote you a note, and in my embarrassment, I handed it to you, and ran away.

Hannah: I don't remember.

Joss: Good.

Hannah: Well, what did it say?

Joss: I have to tell you?

Hannah: Yes. YES!

Joss: Promise you won't hate me?

Hannah: Promise!

Joss: I felt you had such beautiful eyes. So I wrote on the paper, "I love you." And then ran away so you wouldn't see my red face.

Hannah: *(Realizing.)* Oh, that was YOU? My memory must have been playing tricks. I always thought that was Gordon, Gordon Catchpole. Remember him?

Joss: Yes. He beat me up twice. I hated him.

Hannah: And all the time it was YOU that loved me?

Joss: You see, we have been entangled for a very long time. *Macro*-entanglement, you know.

Hannah: That's funny. No, it's more than funny. It's very sweet. Adorable, even.

Joss: When we left Bend we spun off in different directions, you spinning UP. Me spinning DOWN. Yet invisibly connected.

Hannah: I suppose you could say that, by your layman's definition. But just remember, the conservation of energy when entangled particles meet again.

Joss: And that means?

Hannah: All that spinning, up and down; gone. Spooky action at a distance; gone. Entanglement; finished. Just plain old zero state.

Joss: Hah! I didn't know that. Listen, life is coming back to normal. Masks are going away. *(A beat.)* See, over there, the small crowd? There's an open air concert in the park, due to start soon. Looks like a string quartet.

Hannah: I love string music. Especially by Mozart.

Joss: Me too. Shall we go?

Hannah: Sure, I'd like that. Very much.

> *Hannah takes Joss 's arm once more. Joss slowly turns her round so they face each other. She is willing. As he moves to kiss her for the very first time, she responds, very slowly. As their lips touch there is ear-splitting thunder and lightning; then immediately a smash blackout, then silence.*

End of Play.

Family Newspaper

By

John Lane

Family Newspaper was first produced as a staged reading by Drama West at the Barnsdale Art Park, Los Angeles, CA. It was directed by Brian Hutchison and starred Diane Saint-Marie, Alan R. Bemis and Brandon Schwartz.

John Lane is a founding member and former president of New Voices Playwrights Theatre. A retired professor of computer science at California State University, Long Beach, he studied playwriting at South Coast Repertory and sitcom writing at AFI in Los Angeles. Five of his short plays have been published. He has had approximately 40 productions of his short plays in Southern California and nationally, including six in New York City. Although most of his plays are comedies, his long one-act drama *Isosceles* was part of the OC-centric New Play Festival at Chapman University, Orange, Calif.

John Lane is also a member of the Dramatists Guild, Alliance of Los Angeles Playwrights (ALAP) and Orange County Playwrights Alliance (OCPA).

CHARACTERS

Harry, male, 30-35, middle class, dressed casually

Felicia, female, 30-35 middle class, dressed casually

Timmy, male, 9, dressed casually

> *It is early evening in a middle class living room. Harry and Felicia are sitting and reading sections of the newspaper. He is reading the business section; she is reading the news section. Timmy is on the floor reading the newspaper's insert ads. Absorbed in their newspapers and their own agendas, they are barely listening to each other.*

Harry: Damn, they're raising the prime interest rate by a half percent!

Felicia: There's a shoe sale at Nordstrom's.

Harry: *(Getting angry.)* Now our mortgage payment will be going up.

Felicia: Going up? I don't think so. All these shoes are reduced thirty percent. *(Pause.)* I really like those white pumps I got there last year.

Harry: They talk about pumping up the economy. Then the idiots raise the goddamn prime.

Timmy: Geez, they got the new Playstation-4 games in.

Felicia: With these sale prices I'd better be there when they open tomorrow.

Harry: Now there'll be a sell-off when the stock market opens tomorrow.

Timmy: The games are at Best Buy.

Harry: When the prime goes up, the market always reacts. Those bastards, they always announce bad news when the market is closed.

Felicia: I'm sure the market's open until midnight, dear. I know Safeway is open.

Timmy: Wow, what cool games. Look, they got Vicious Venomous Vipers in. Can I get it, Dad?

Felicia: And the selections. *(Rhapsodizes.)* Shoes from Spain, from Brazil, from Italy... I just love Italian shoes.

Timmy: Mom, it's at Best Buy.

Felicia: *(Impatiently.)* Timmy, they don't sell shoes at Best Buy. The sale's at Nordstrom's.

Harry: *(Fuming.)* Everything's going up. Next thing it will be the damned sales tax. It's already seven and a half or something.

Felicia: Don't be silly, dear. I could never get into a seven and a half shoe. *(Coyly.)* Although, I suppose I could've in my prime.

Harry: That's exactly my point. There was no need to <u>raise</u> the prime. The economy's basically sound.

Timmy: The games are all on sale the Saturday.

Felicia: *(Turns to Harry.)* Harry, why don't you take him to his game on Saturday? You haven't seen him play all season.

Harry: I thought soccer was over.

Felicia: Must be the summer league. *(Raises voice.)* It <u>is</u> the summer league, isn't it, Timmy?

Timmy: There's no league in summer, mom. *(Impatiently changing the subject.)* Dad, it's the Venomous Vipers game. I saw it on TV. It's so cool.

Harry: Venomous Vipers? Is that what they're using for team names nowadays? Whatever happened to team names like the Tigers and Lions and Impalas?

Felicia: *(Whiny.)* You're out of touch, Harry. These are the names that young people relate to. Frankly, I like the sound of "Vipers".

Harry: Soccer's a running game, Felicia. Vipers don't run. They crawl or something. Lions and Impalas run.

Timmy: It's a cool game, Mom. Can I get it on CD?

Harry: That's another thing. Watch the six-month CD rates go up next week at the bank. All because of one man. One man decides when the prime is to go up!

Felicia: What man? Who are you talking about, Harry?

Harry: *(Still angry.)* That Fed guy... used to be Alan Greenspan. I don't know who it is now.

Timmy: Mom! Dad! My game... what about my game?

Felicia: *(Whiny voice to Harry.)* It's always me taking him to his games. It would be nice if his <u>father</u> could watch him play once in a while.

Harry: When did you say it was? Saturday? I have golf that day.

Felicia: Who with? This Alan-what's-his-name? Harry, is it really necessary to do business on Saturday? Saturday should be for family.

Timmy: Mom, I'm talking about this video game. There's no soccer.

Felicia: They called it off? It's just as well. They shouldn't have you playing in this heat.

Harry: An overheated economy... I suppose that's their official rationale for raising the interest.

Felicia: Exactly my point, Harry. Show more interest in his activities. The other fathers are there every Saturday watching their sons play. And how do you suppose that makes <u>him</u> feel when his <u>own</u> father is out somewhere on a golf course with this Alan-what's-his-name? Alan...

Harry: Greenspan. Used to be Greenspan. I forget who it is now. I don't play golf with him!

Felicia: *(Pause.)* Green-whatever. *(Pause.)* That reminds me; I could use some Green flats to go with my new pantsuit. I might as well take advantage of this sale.

Timmy: I haven't got any new games since my birthday. Come on, Mom. They're on sale.

Felicia: The sale starts at nine tomorrow.

Timmy: It's not 'til Saturday.

Felicia: I'm talking about Nordstrom's, Timmy.

Timmy: They have Playstation-4 games at Nordstrom's?

Felicia: No, Honey, they have shoes at Nordstrom's. Shoes!

Harry: Didn't he just get shoes for his birthday?

Timmy: Yeah, I got soccer shoes; and one video game. And that was the last time I got <u>any</u> games.

Harry: If you played your last game, then you don't need new soccer shoes. *(Pause.)* That settles that.

> *Harry puts down his paper and looks at Felicia.*

Are you through with the front section, Felicia?

> *Harry and Felicia exchange newspaper sections. They each browse through a few pages.*

Timmy: *(Exasperated.)* Hey, are you guys listening to me? I said video games. Video, video, video!

Felicia: What was the name of that movie coming out, Harry? The one with Tom Cruise. It's out on video this week.

Harry: I don't know; something about a...

Felicia: Yes, we really ought to rent it. I wonder if Netflix has it available yet.

Timmy: Hey, they have my game at Best Buy, too. Can we go?

Harry: I can't think of the name of the film. Something like...

Timmy: *(Impatiently.)* Vicious Venomous Vipers!

Felicia: No, Timmy, that sounds like a porn movie. Tom Cruise wouldn't be in a porn movie.

Harry: Alright, young man! Where have you been getting porno? *(To Felicia.)* This is what happens when they cancel summer soccer.

Felicia: If you'd spend more time with him, Harry...

Harry: Felicia, the kid hasn't even shaved yet. He shouldn't be interested in porno. And believe me, I'm going to have a talk with that guy at the Best Buy.

Felicia: Best Buy doesn't carry porno, Harry. It's against their policy.

Harry: I never liked the looks of that clerk there. You know, the balding guy with the rimless glasses. I bet he's dealing porno videos from under the counter.

Timmy: Can I get it then? When we go to Best Buy? My video?

Harry: you're not getting any porno films, young man. And that's final! You're much too young.

Felicia: Timmy, why can't you be interested in things your own age. Things like... games.

Harry: Yes, those Playstation games. They develop good motor skills and you'll have good, clean, harmless fun blowing up tiny alien creatures.

Timmy: I want the Vipers game. Vipers aren't tiny alien creatures, Dad.

Felicia: *(Fatherly advice.)* The important thing is that vipers are evil, Timmy. You'll be destroying evil things. That's what you learn from these games.

Timmy: Then I can get it?

Felicia: Yes, I suppose so. We'll go on Saturday. It will take your mind off porno.

Timmy: Wow! Cool! *(Pause.)* Dad, can I have the sports section?

> *Harry finds the sports section and hands it to Timmy, then continues browsing through the news section.*

Harry: Hmm, there's a shoe sale at Nordstrom's. Felicia. *(Pause.)* Those black loafers of mine are a bit beat up, don't you think? I ought to pick up a couple of pairs.

Felicia: And while you're at it, shy not pick up a pair of golfing shoes. Yours are pretty worn. *(Pause.)* You can use the new ones the next time you gold with your friend, that Alan-what's-his-name... Greenpeace.

Harry: Not "peace', Felicia. "Span". Greenspan! And he's not my friend.

Timmy: Those Greenpeace guys have a neat boat, and they save whales.

Felicia: Timmy, we're not talking about whales. We're talking about golf.

Harry: Greenpeace, Greenspan... enough about Greenspan.

Felicia: *(Looking at the newspaper.)* Something here about an interest rate. *(Pause.)* Harry, do you suppose that will affect our credit cards? You ought to talk to Greenspan about it the next time you two play golf.

Harry: We do have a credit card for Nordstrom's, don't we? I need to get those shoes.

Felicia: It's criminal what they charge for interest on those credit cards.

Harry: Felicia, I was talking about shoes!

Felicia: Well, I'm talking about interest rates!

Timmy: *(Reading the sports section.)* Gee, look at the standings. The Dodgers are only half a game behind.

Felicia: I don't understand that, Harry. How can they be a half game behind? Do they quit in the middle of a game or something? I think they should always finish the game.

Harry: It's the math, Felicia. It's the way they figure it. It depends on wins and losses.

Felicia: They should finish the game. What kind of message are they sending to young people?

Timmy: Gee, Dad, tomorrow night at the Dodger's game they're giving away free plastic bats.

Harry: It's not really free, Timmy. You still have to pay to get into the game.

Felicia: I thought the game was Saturday. Or did you say they cancelled it?

Harry: They cancelled soccer. They never cancel baseball; except of course for rain.

Timmy: The game's tomorrow.

Felicia: Nordstrom's sale is tomorrow.

Timmy: They're playing the Diamondbacks.

Felicia: Diamondbacks? Aren't those snakes?

Timmy: Yeah, snakes; just like vipers. Vipers are snakes.

Felicia: Then why didn't they name them Vipers? It's a much classier name.

Timmy: My Vicious Venomous Vipers game; wait 'til I get it, Mom. It's so cool!

Felicia: I don't care for baseball. It's so slow, and I never understand what's going on.

Timmy: I'm talking about my new video game, Mom. At Best Buy.

Felicia: That reminds me; we've got to get that new Tom Cruise video.

Harry: Maybe we can get it at Best Buy.

Felicia: Yes, and then Timmy can pick up his free plastic bat.

Timmy: Best Buy doesn't give out free bats.

Felicia: What <u>is</u> the name of that Tom Cruise movie? It's on the tip of my tongue.

Harry: About that shoe sale, Felicia, we should get there early.

Felicia: Yes, before the interest rates go up.

Harry: *(Pause.)* Well, as long as we get my shoes.

> *Timmy, disgusted, looks at Harry and Felicia and shakes his head as they continue reading. Blackout.*

End of play

The Gifting

By

Fengar Gael

The Gifting has been developed in conjunction with New Voices Playwrights Theatre, Orange County, CA.

Fengar Gael has had readings, workshops, and productions at the Sundance Theatre Lab, Utah Shakespearean Festival, the InterAct Theatre of Philadelphia, New Jersey Repertory, Playwrights Theatre of New Jersey, Detroit Repertory Theatre, the Salt Lake Acting Company, the Moxie Theatre of San Diego, The Kitchen Dog Theatre of Dallas, The Irish Theatre of Chicago, the Botanicum Seedlings of Topanga, California, Harlequin Productions of Auburn New York, the Rorschach Theatre of D.C., the Venus Theatre of Laurel, Maryland, and in New York City: Playwrights Gallery, Urban Stages, MultiStages, the Abingdon Theatre, The Secret Theatre, The Spiral Theatre, Collaborative Arts Project 21, Turn to Flesh Productions, The Resonance Ensemble Theatre, Medicine Show Theatre, The Identity Theater, Yonder Window Theatre, and Ego Actus Theatre.

She is a recipient of the Craig Noel Award (for *Devil Dog Six*), the Playwrights First Award (for *Opaline*), Manhattan Theatre Works Excellence in Playwriting Award (for *The Draper*); and commissions from South Coast Repertory, the Hangar Theatre, New Jersey Repertory, and the InterAct Theatre (through the National New Play Network), and a playwriting fellowship from the California Arts Council.

For more information visit: www.fengar.com

The Gifting

CHARACTERS

Clive Granville, a middle-aged London gallerist

Mavis Fortescue, a middle-aged London barrister

> *It is the present. A stylized set suggests a parlor of a stately home in London where Grecian goddess statues are among the furnishings or supplied by the imaginations of the audience. A bell chimes as CLIVE GRANVILLE answers the door to his elegant parlor decorated with Grecian statues. MAVIS FORTESCUE, a fastidiously dressed barrister, enters brandishing a pistol.*

Mavis: You Judas! You bastard! You sodding son of a bitch!

Clive: Good to see you too, Mavis. You're not seriously going to shoot...?

Mavis: If I don't, I'll have you arrested! I'll see your gallery disgraced; your reputation ruined!

Clive: I was waiting to hear from you.

Mavis: It's bad enough you stole Charlotte's work, work which rightfully belongs to me, but to display it in your gallery under a false name the unmitigated gall! You're shameless! You've no conscience! No scruples!

Clive: No need to get hysterical; now please let me explain.

Mavis: Oh, you'll explain all right; to the judge, jury, and the whole bloody world when I expose you as the deceitful, lying rotter that you are!

Clive: Give me five minutes, just five minutes.

Mavis: I've been to the gallery! I've seen them with my own eyes! They're hers, which means they're mine. She willed her sculptures to me... all of them!

Clive: Well, yes, you're her sister, but those are not her sculptures. I admit they're similar but they're mine. I made them and used another name.

Mavis: You!? You can't sculpt! You can't even draw! *(Gesturing to several statues.)* What are these doing here?! She willed them to me. They're mine!

Clive: You can have them, every one! I'll give you anything you want if you'll hear me out.

Mavis: How do you live with yourself?!

Clive: Charlotte gave me her hands.

Mavis: What?!

Clive: When Charlotte spoke her last words, she said, "Will you take my hands?" Naturally, I thought she was asking if I'd take her hands in my own, if I'd hold and caress them, but she was really asking if I'd take what they can do, what they can feel and create. You see, when we touched she truly gave me her hands; so now I can do what Charlotte could do! It's her gift to me, and it's changed my life.

Mavis: My god...

Mavis sighs, pocketing the pistol.

The Gifting

Clive: Oh, I know it sounds preposterous, but remember when Charlotte and I gave our first dinner party, the week after we married?

Mavis: No.

Clive: I was chopping chilies but was so blotto the knife slipped and slashed the tendons on all four fingers of my left hand... bloody awful mess. Surely you remember.

Mavis: Vaguely.

Clive: Two doctors spent three hours stitching me up, and after that my chance to experience the world through touch was diminished – until now. I didn't realize it until hours later when I felt a strange tingling, and look! *(Fluttering his fingers.)* A concert pianist couldn't ask for better mobility!

Mavis: Stand back, dammit!

Clive: Naturally, it struck me as portentous to suddenly, on the very night Charlotte passed away, to have my touch back, so the next day I went straight to Doctor Curry who called it a minor miracle, a gift of spontaneous healing. That's when it occurred to me, when he said "gift", that's when I remembered Charlotte saying, "take my hands," and that's when she gave me her gift.

Mavis: My god, I've never heard such rubbish! And don't tell me you're so grief stricken you've lost your mind!

Clive: Ha! Very nearly, because after this resurgence of feeling, the hands became restless, the digits wanted to dance, tippity-tap-tap! Skimming surfaces, stroking textures, they possessed a will of their own, a will to create!

The Gifting

Mavis: I hope this isn't the story you're going to tell the police.

Clive: Why not? It's true! I suppose you think it's ironic that Charlotte gave her gift to me.

Mavis: What I think is that the trauma of losing her has affected your mind, and this is your perverse way of bringing her back.

Clive: Look at me, Mavis, a man my age doesn't suddenly find himself in the thrall of a talent he's never even aspired to. When I wanted to be an artist, it was a painter, then a composer, and briefly even a poet, but never a sculptor. This gift is from Charlotte. Charlotte had powers, incredible, unspeakable powers. How can I make you believe me?

Mavis: You can't!

Clive: But look at my draped damsels, my swagged hags, ha! I can weld, mix and mold. I brandish chisels, files, and rasps; and slowly, very slowly, I'm introducing my work into various nooks in the gallery. I'm calling myself Charles Lott in honor of Charlotte. Rather clever, don't you think?

Mavis: What I think is that you need help; immediate psychiatric help! Everything you've said strikes me as dead wrong, unscrupulous, and unjust to Charlotte.

Clive: What about me? It's exhausting being enslaved to her hands, all her frills and flounces looping this way and that. Of course, it's marvelous just to be able to do it, but I haven't slept more than three hours a night. The trouble is I'm mostly on my feet...

Mavis: And off your trolley! Listen, Clive, people can't pass talent like a tray of hors oeuvres. Talent stems from heredity, craftsmanship, years of arduous labor. What you've done is hoard her sculpture; sculptures that should have been loaded on a lorry and brought to me six months ago! But you won't get away with it! I won't let you steal the glory which by rights belongs to Charlotte. She never even had her bloody fifteen minutes.

Clive: She didn't miss much.

Mavis: I've met with my solicitor and assuming I don't shoot you, you can expect to be arrested by the end of the week.

Clive: Arrested?!

Mavis: Then you'll be arraigned, prosecuted, and confined at Sudbury Prison.

Clive: Prison?!

Mavis: I'm also filing a civil suit.

Clive: You're what?!

Mavis: By April the gallery will be closed...

Clive: No!

Mavis: ...your property confiscated...

Clive: Oh, Mavis...

Mavis: ...you'll be bankrupt!

Clive: I never knew you could be so vengeful. You really want to ruin me?

Mavis: You'll manage. Parolees are placed in various trades.

Clive: Trades?!

Mavis: Pressing laundry, stuffing sausages...

Clive: Oh, god...

Mavis: ...cleaning latrines...

Clive: How can I make you see?!

Mavis: You can't!

Clive: Ah! I know; I'll prove it! I'll demonstrate; I'll sketch your portrait!

Clive snatches a sketch pad and pencil.

The least you can do before wrecking my life is give me three more minutes, just three. Now sit! Sit in that chair.

Mavis: I will not!

Clive: Then stand! *(Sketching at a manic pace.)* Look how deftly I'm drawing! Charlotte said a good sculptor must above all be a good draftsman, capable of generating lines, and not just any old lines, but lines that lead towards depth. Think of it: without depth we'd all be exposed, our features flattened like platters. Let's take your nose for instance: the flawless Fortescue nose! It's juxtaposition to the lachrymal fossa at the corner of the eyes is purest poetry. And now I'm drawing your ear! More than any feature, it varies infinitely, and as a rule the measurement from ear to ear equals the measurement from chin to brow. Don't move! I keep wondering: if I have Charlotte's hands, do I also have her brain? I mean, our tactile feelings are mapped onto our minds from infancy, so really, I'm a child again. I even removed the signs in the gallery that said "Don't Touch" because they might as well be saying, don't feel, don't breathe, drop dead!

Mavis: That's it! Enough!

Clive: Wait!

Clive whips his sketch off the pad and waves it.

Voila!

Pause as Mavis snatches the portrait and stares.

Well...? Now do you believe me? It's your face, the way Charlotte would have drawn it!

Mavis: *(Pause, collecting herself.)* Yes... yes, it is. Apparently, losing Charlotte has caused more than a breakdown; it's caused a breakthrough to your own talent. You've repressed it all these years and now it's finally emerged, but don't deceive yourself; it's a rip off, and you're nothing but a degenerate thief!

Clive: But at least you believe these sculptures are mine!

Mavis: It's... possible.

Clive: Let me take you to the studio; let me show you how I work!

Mavis: Even if you convince me, you're still just a copyist, a trifling forger who's appropriated the style of a woman you lived with for twenty years and never thought worthy of a single solitary exhibit!

Clive: That's not true; it's not that simple. The trouble with you Mavis is you've never appreciated my position.

Mavis: I most certainly have. You're a demigod! You proclaim, "The Chosen," then they're instantly exalted, make heaps of money, while Charlotte languished in utter obscurity.

Clive: Dealers who exhibit the work of their wives are perceived as nepotistic, and the wives are invariably subjected to ridicule. It's a conflict of interest, a question of honor.

Mavis: It's not honor; it's fear of the petty prejudices of petty people, all of whom you value more than you ever valued Charlotte, which is why she left all her sculptures to me!

Clive: You're her sister!

Mavis: And I'll do all I can to make the whole world see how splendid they are.

Clive: Believe me, Mavis, the world sees what it's told to see and how, and it won't give a damn about Charlotte and her sculptures.

Mavis: Then I'll tell them; I'll show them.

The Gifting

Clive: Where and with whom? Besides, most dealers can't tell a work of art from a butchered cow. Truth be told, the art world's a swamp of faddist toads who can't see beyond what's hyped or most likely to induce vomiting.

Mavis: You're the toad, Clive; you're the king of toads!

Clive: Look, Mavis, can't we be more civil? This isn't easy on either of us; and you're wrong about Charlotte. She preferred obscurity. Recognition only matters if you question your worth, and Charlotte never did.

Mavis: You supercilious ass! What do you think destroyed and devoured her? Doubt, the pain and poison of doubt!

Clive: What melodramatic drivel! What Charlotte had was cancer; very simple. The cancer won and that's that. If she had doubts, she never stopped working long enough to indulge them; and stop looking so bloody sanctimonious! What did you ever do for her career?

Mavis: I praised her, encouraged her, took a genuine interest.

Clive: And how many sculptures did that sell? I once told Charlotte the art world would need a seismic leap of taste for her work to be accepted much less esteemed. Now I'm learning it first-hand since I haven't sold a single piece.

Mavis: Good! Because I won't stand idly by, while you profit from her work.

Clive: I never expected you to. I was hoping we'd share the profits.

Mavis: What?!

Clive: Well, why not? I know you need the money. Charlotte told me about your investment. Sussex poultry, wasn't it?

Mavis: None of your damn business!

Clive: The point is, once I convince the public to appreciate the statues, we could make a tidy fortune.

Mavis: *(Pause.)* God, you never cease to amaze me, and to think I once admired you. You're the vainest, most repulsive man I've ever met!

Clive: Look, Mavis, I don't expect you to like me, but perhaps you might learn to tolerate me, or at least tolerate my creations. Look, here, my very own Pandora. From a distance, she's light as pastry, and yet when you touch... Oh, please touch her. Charlotte said her sculptures could be used as a kind of meditation. She wanted people to touch them, to lose themselves in the hills and hollows.

> *A haunting melody is heard as Mavis succumbs to the sensuous forms, stroking Pandora's curves.*

You'll find they're very... consoling. Every fold has a life of its own, especially when it loses its moorings, casting wayward shadows; like that playful one on her thigh.

Mavis: The fabric seems as alive as the flesh. Oh, lord, my... my knees have gone wobbly.

Clive: Sit down; I'll fix some drinks.

> *Clive opens a cabinet and pours two brandies.*

Mavis: I can see why you cling to your delusion, but even if Charlotte did have the power to pass on her talent, she'd never have passed it to you.

Clive: I can't explain that. All I know is we've suffered a tragic loss, but believe me, Mavis, the gift of Charlotte redeems the loss.

Mavis: No, no, it doesn't. Nothing redeems the loss.

Clive: True, I... I only meant it makes it... bearable.

Mavis: Does it really? Then give me the hands!

Mavis grasps Clive's hands.

Ouch!! Now say what Charlotte said to you! Speak up, dammit! Say the words!

Clive: I... I said, "Won't you..."

Mavis: Go on!

Clive: "Won't you take my hands?"

Mavis: Yes! Yes, I'll take your hands! Ha, ha!

MAVIS feels the power of the hands passing into her own. SHE gasps with rapturous joy, then releases CLIVE'S hands.

Ha, ha! Ha, ha, ha!

MAVIS laughs with glee, fluttering her fingers while CLIVE weeps.

Clive: No, nooooooo...

Mavis: Yessss!

<u>End of play</u>

Lucky Two-Dollar Bill

By

David Rusiecki

David Rusiecki is the president of the New Voices Playwrights Theatre. A member since 2009, he has contributed to New Voices Playwrights Theatre as a writer, director, actor and co-producer. He has also served as head of the New Works Festival Literary Committee and Board of Trustees with the Long Beach Playhouse. His full-length *Sides* was selected for the Long Beach Playhouse New Works table-read series while in the same year *...Prep...* received honorable mention with Panndora Productions' annual festival of new play readings. His one-act play *Kid Gloves* (originally entitled *Have A Nice Day*) has been published in <u>The Best American Short Plays 2012-2013</u> (Applause Books) as well as in <u>Best Monologues from Best American Short Plays</u> (Applause Books). His one-act play *Long Time Coming* has been published in <u>The Best American Short Plays 2014-2015</u> (Applause Books). Other one-act plays produced by New Voices Playwrights Theatre include *Mistle-in-Tow* at STAGEStheatre (Fullerton, CA) along with *Two-Some, A Fake Christmas, The Big 3-0, $ecret $anta, Long Time Coming, Holiday Hoo-Ha, Return To Sender, Have a Nice Day,* and *Last Call* at Stage Door Repertory Theatre (Anaheim, CA). Other full-length works which received staged readings include *Groupie* at Theatre Out (Santa Ana, CA) as well as *Scattered Showers, The Wrecking Ball* and *Goon* at Stage Door Repertory Theatre. He can be reached at: <u>djrusiecki@gmail.com</u>

CHARACTERS

Patti, female, 30s

Chatterbox One, female, 30s

Chatterbox Two, female, 30s

Everyone Else, various voices in age and gender

> *Lights rise on Patti sitting and talking on a
> video chat. She is at home.*

Patti: *(To audience.)* So, I go this particular grocery
store in the area, close to home where I like their
selection of beef loin. Of locally grown white corn. My
husband prefers another place, he's a little more finicky
about where we get our food for dinner. Anyway I go
there and I get approached by some woman right
outside the entrance. She seems young, mid-twenties.
Perhaps younger. Very stunning facial features. With
long black hair, but most importantly with a two-year
old in tow. The baby has curly, sandy-blondish hair. It's
my first time seeing them here. This woman greets me
as I'm about to enter pushing my cart and begins telling
me how they're not homeless but that she just lost her
job and is asking me for anything to help out.
Basically, a beggar. But she had this accent… maybe
Middle Eastern or soft Russian? I'm not really good
with identifying those kind of things when it comes to
certain ethnicities. And it's not like she's carrying a
cardboard sign or anything. That kind you see at traffic
lights collecting spare cash from motorists. Those
people are really worse off. But somehow, she and her
daughter don't look as desperate as the rest. She's very
apologetic, very friendly, very modest. My heart just

goes out to her, you know? I mean, they both seem harmless enough. So I pull out a two-dollar bill from my purse. Yes, they still make two-dollar bills. It's a tradition in my family at Lunar New Year... we pass Lucky Money, as they call it, around to family members. Everyone starts the New Year with a crisp lucky two-dollar bill. So I had a leftover one still in fresh condition, I take the bill from my purse and gave it her. Hopefully that will give her some luck. And I explain it's the only cash I have and wish them the best. She smiles... feebly then turns away. It was such an awkward encounter; I didn't know what to make of it. Anyway, I go inside the store and just as I turn around, her daughter lets out this high-pitched cry. Practically everyone in the store notices. And right at that moment, I see the two of them about to advance towards someone else. Now, of course, I didn't know if she made her baby cry on purpose to gather sympathy from that other person. I say that because... I mean, her baby just like that began screaming nonstop. Almost on cue. Like I said, her baby was fine when they came up to me, but I can't help but think like somehow... she agitated the baby before approaching anyone else. And no, I'm not going to take a picture. I feel bad for the child as it is. But in all honesty, I don't know what to believe anymore. So, I get home and go online to our public community page to post my experience. Basically to see if anyone has ever come across these particular people at that store. And then, all hell breaks loose...

Chatterbox One and Two appear on screen.

Chatterbox One: Oh my God, they're <u>always</u> around there.

Patti: They <u>are</u>?

Chatterbox Two: I also see them hanging out at Target.

Patti: You have?

Chatterbox One: Of course, this is what they do daily. They move around where they can't be caught. In fact, I just saw that same woman you're describing at the post office on Monday. She was doing the exact same thing with her daughter!

Patti: Come on.

Chatterbox One: I'm serious. I was there for about forty-five minutes trying to get a new passport. As I was leaving a police car pulled up and they quickly bolted.

Patti: Wow, I had no idea.

Chatterbox Two: The police should always be called if you have even the slightest inkling a child is being abused, trafficked, mistreated.

Patti: But, I mean… asking me for money, I really wouldn't consider child abuse.

Chatterbox One: But using a child to get money in this way is. Not to mention anything else that could be going on.

Patti: I still don't know.

Chatterbox Two: With trafficking going on, unlivable conditions, malnutrition… all that. You need to contact CPS. I can give you the hotline number.

Patti: You sure? That seems a bit extreme.

Chatterbox One: Protect children no matter what.

Patti: (*To audience.*) So there I was... stuck in this conundrum. But it just got worse.

Chatterbox One: They're gypsies, you know.

Patti: Huh?

Chatterbox Two: Someone told me a couple years back these people are 'gypsies.' And the kids they drag around with them… aren't even theirs.

Patti: You're kidding me.

Chatterbox One: They trade them off to others who stand outside Target, Walmart, Costco, etc. It's all a business to them. You better wake up.

Patti: I'm not gonna bother calling the cops or foster care. I mean, why would they want to take any case without solid information. Besides it's just so… you know, so heart-breaking to see all this.

Chatterbox One: We're telling you, call CPS.

Chatterbox Two: If it turns out this woman and her so-called kid didn't actually need help then just think, one day it'll come back to bite them.

Patti: But I want to help.

Chatterbox One: We all do. I'm just telling you… believe nothing.

Patti: Really?

Chatterbox Two: If you see them again, look around carefully. You will see a man sitting in an SUV watching them very closely. That man is her handler. Most of the time these women are also sex trafficking victims. The child is most likely borrowed or rented. The child is there to gain sympathy from you. It's all just a scam.

Patti: Are you sure?

Chatterbox One: I'll say it again, these people are gypsies. They are a network. This is how they make their living.

Patti: But she had such a pretty face… why would she engage in this sort of nefarious activity?

Chatterbox Two: Because at first glance, it seems poor and unfortunate, but when you really understand the scam behind their system, it's absolutely disgusting. I have no respect for these peoples way of life, and of course it's terrible for the children that are rented and borrowed and the women are sex trafficked but all gypsies answer to a larger mafia.

Patti: You're kidding.

Chatterbox One: She switches it up with the children. In fact, I've seen her with infants, toddlers, all the way up to pre-teen.

Patti: I can't believe this.

Chatterbox Two: I once saw her pushing a stroller outside Kohl's two days ago. She said the same thing to me, but I told her I no longer carry any cash. Later on I saw a man pick them up in a Mercedes or some other luxury car.

Patti: And this is how she lives?

Chatterbox One: Very comfortably.

Patti: You know this for absolute certain?

Chatterbox Two: I see all this. We all do. You just happened to catch on later than others. Just face it, you got scammed.

Chatterbox One: I remember seeing a community of people like them in England and Spain. A train conductor warned travelers to be careful because there was a group getting on the train. You get to see the gypsy way of life and culture in those countries, there was a serious divide between the gypsies and the regular citizens. It's no different here just on a smaller scale.

Patti: I'm sorry… I mean, I've heard of a few stories, but how can we really know for sure what the difference is between a homeless person and gypsy at first glance?

Chatterbox Two: Consider the possibility you really don't know and you really aren't likely to know her truth. If two-dollars is that big a deal, don't give it next time. Even if this woman is conning you, who cares? No need to complain.

Patti: Look, I'm not complaining. I think you're misinterpreting my original post. I gave her my two-dollar bill, no one forced me. She definitely did not. My hand did not just automatically decide to give money against my thoughts. It's more of a question of one's integrity. And all of a sudden, I'm now wondering if she truly is a gypsy as everyone else seems to say so. I know to keep an eye out for her in the future. And I worry for the child, but my biggest fault in all this is… okay, what if I do call CPS and risk putting a child into the system that let's say, isn't the greatest? Perhaps she really is a struggling mom and a move on my part takes her child away from her. Apparently people here on this community group are thinking everyone is biased or has an agenda. I get it, we're all tired of the drama and hate. But I am a Person of Color and I get it all the time. I just want to know, did I do my part to help a child get fed no matter how minimal it was?

Pause as Chatterbox One and Two disappear.

(*To audience.*) Then I realized, I wish I hadn't said all that. Because for the next twelve hours, my feed was flooded with all these comments from people I've never met in my life. And most of it was downright offensive. I mean…yes, I could have kept this to myself. But part of me does care. A big part. And now I'm being shamed into keeping my mouth shut and my opinions to myself. Not so much my opinions but even saying one word can get in caught up in a mess you never wanted in the first place.

Everyone Else, Chatterbox One and Two appear.

And thus, the avalanche of pushback began…

Everyone Else: So everyone with a child is on welfare? Huge misconception right there.

Chatterbox One: She doesn't need to beg if she is eligible for aide, she's just scamming everyone.

Chatterbox Two: You'll even see some guy playing the violin outside of Sprouts. It's fraud. He's gypsy too. He's not really playing, it's attached to a recording. If you watch you can tell what he is "playing" doesn't match the music.

Chatterbox One: Don't be upset that you did what you thought was right. They are wrong and will have to deal with the consequences of being dishonest.

Everyone Else: I'd buy them a sandwich but for heaven's sake, don't give them money.

Chatterbox One: That's what I was going to say. I never give cash, but will ask what it is they might need from the store for two dollars, five dollars or whatever amount they're asking for.

Chatterbox Two: One-hundred percent with you.

Everyone Else: Direct them to social services or the Mayor's office. There is help available funded by our taxes.

Chatterbox One: She probably had a brand new minivan parked around the corner.

Chatterbox Two: I watched a gypsy walk to hers after panhandling with three…count 'em, three kids in tow.

Everyone Else: Definitely gypsies. It's a trope that has been going around for decades. You said it almost verbatim.

Chatterbox One: Men make them beg. So tragic.

Chatterbox Two: As others said, very likely a panhandler. You can call the non-emergency police line for a welfare check on that child.

Everyone Else: Buy her a banana. I ask if they want a piece of fruit or an energy bar. Costs nothing, and weeds out the ones that are really hungry vs. the imposters. Pay it forward.

Chatterbox One: It's a network it's what they do as a community as a whole. They use every government program and panhandle in every city that allows it.

Chatterbox Two: If you really want to make a difference, give your money to legit organizations that are fighting the war on sex trafficking and addiction. By giving to people like this, you are perpetuating this panhandling activity in our city.

Everyone Else: Bunch of gypsy pimps all over the place.

Chatterbox One: Stop giving these people cash!

Chatterbox Two: They're still people, still oppressed, still need our help.

Everyone Else, Chatterbox One and Two exit.

Patti: (*To audience.*) And so this went on for hours, stretching out to a couple of days. I never anticipated anything like it. I didn't realize I had hit a nerve with these people. But I stopped looking at the comments. They just digressed into the lowest form of communicating. Some truly revolting personal comments, completely unnecessary. I had read enough, I won't be logging on to that community page any time soon. I mean, I never meant to bring this topic up like that. It was only an observation… it wasn't supposed to go off the rails, but it did. And now, here I am more confused than before. Never did I realize that a two-dollar bill in my purse which I rarely ever use would cause such an unnecessary commotion… maybe it's not-so-lucky after all.

Lights fade as we see Patti close out her screen.

__End of play.__

Memories of Big Papa

By

Lillian Nader

Lillian Nader, M.Ed., is a novelist, playwright, and copyeditor living in Southern California. In retrospect, Lillian admits to spending too many years teaching when she could have been writing plays. Her book, *Theep and Thorpe: Adventures in Space*, is a science fiction novel for young readers. Lillian is a contributing author to the e-book *Muse & Ink: Soul Expressions Through Writing*. Other publications include educational workbooks on cooperative learning in the classroom. Two of her short plays have been published in New Voices Playwrights Theatre anthologies. Back when live theater was a thing, her short holiday play, *Blue Hair & Rap*, was premiered at Stage Door Repertory Theatre in Anaheim, CA. She is currently writing a full-length musical play based on mythology.

CHARACTERS

Narrator, female, 70, of Lebanese descent. She speaks with a slight Southern accent. She uses different voices to portray family members:

Ron, male, as a young boy in East Texas

Big Papa, male, gruff voice with Lebanese accent

Asma, female, melancholy voice, Lebanese accent

Big Papa's father, male, middle-aged, speaks with Lebanese accent

Cousin Raymond, male as a young boy from Texas

Aunt Maine, female, 30s with Southern accent

Cousin Paula, female, 16 with Southern accent.

Cousin Suzanne, female, 40s with Southern accent

Monologue.

> _The tone is nostalgic. The narrator recalls conversations and events with her brother and cousins as they share fond memories of their grandfather._

Narrator: Nostalgia can conjure mixed feelings. For some, it evokes warm memories of childhood antics and family gatherings. Others suffer deep emotions of loss when they reminisce. They regret that happy days with a deceased relative can't be repeated. It's important to capture the memories of living relatives when we have a chance and record our oral history for future generations. Fortunately, I have no regrets when I think of my Big Papa. (Pause.) Back when *The Reader's Digest* was a household object, Big Papa read it in Arabic. Big Papa was my mother's Papa and someone my big brother, Ron, looked up to. He stood six feet tall and weighed 200 pounds... mostly muscle. Once, while on a visit with Big Papa in Lake Charles, Ron saw him turning the pages a different way while reading *The Reader's Digest.* Arabic is printed from right to left.

Voice of Ron: Why do you read like that, Big Papa? I read the opposite way in English.

Narrator: Big Papa replied…

Voice of Big Papa: We were here first!

Narrator: We read *The Reader's Digest* in English in my home when I was growing up. "My Most Unforgettable Character" was a regular feature. Today, I would choose my Big Papa as both unforgettable and definitely a character! My grandfather, George Asaff, was a native of Berbara, Lebanon, a village near Beirut. He was born on August 6, 1889, and his wife, Asma, was born in 1890. George and Asma were married when he was about twenty, and she, nineteen. They immigrated to the US in 1911. George came to America first to earn money to send for Asma and their baby, Matilda. That baby was my mother. When asked why they left the old country, Asma would say…

Voice of Asma: Our people were starving.

Narrator: As a boy in Lebanon, George was conscripted by the Ottoman Empire to secure food for the Turkish army. He rarely spoke of those days, but my brother spent a lot of time with him on fishing trips. One day while they were fishing, Big Papa lit up a cigarette. *Yuck*, thought Ron.

Voice of Ron: Big Papa, why did you ever start smoking?

Voice of Big Papa: To light da fuses.

Voice of Ron: What fuses?

Voice of Big Papa: Dynamite fuses. Da Turks make me gather fish killed by the dynamite. I fool them. I put the big fish under a rock and get it later.

Narrator: Big Papa didn't mention how risky it was for him to take fish home to his family. But he did tell Ron about coming to America. His father already lived here, and George asked him to send money so he could join him.

Voice of Big Papa's father: I send money only when you marry. You must prove you are reliable and plan to settle down in the new country.

Voice of Big Papa: So, I go from village to village to find woman to marry. Asma was the one I like, and I already know her.

Narrator: Big Papa went fishing and always caught a lot. He would drive up the driveway, stop under the kitchen window, honk, and yell…

Voice of Big Papa: Woman, get da knife and da pan!

Narrator: When we would tell Big Mama that was not right, she just smiled and started cleaning. She never forgot how hard things were back in the old country. In the United States, her husband brought the fish home without risking his life. Asma knew what her job was, and she was thankful for it. (*Pause.*) George became a naturalized citizen in 1924. Although he could not read or write English, his teenage daughter, Matilda, helped him prepare for his naturalization exam and sign his name in English. In his back yard in Lake Charles, Louisiana, George built a candy kitchen and made delicious peanut brittle by hand in copper kettles. He peddled candy, linen, and Dan River fabrics from the trunk of his car. When he needed to stay overnight, he would say to a client:

Voice of Big Papa: I give you these nice pillowcases for a place to sleep.

Narrator: His customers were happy to accommodate. (*Pause.*) My cousin, Jerry Asaff, went to Lamar University in Beaumont, Texas. As a pledge in a fraternity, the upperclassmen put him and two others in a car trunk, took them into Louisiana, and dropped them off in a secluded area that looked like a swamp. They walked for a very long time before they saw a house. The porch light was on, so they knocked on the door and asked to use the phone. Once inside, they introduced themselves. When Jerry said his name was Asaff, they asked him if he was related to The Chief. When he told them that people referred to his grandfather as the chief, they offered them food and gave them some money so the boys could play poker with them. What a stroke of luck for Jerry to be stranded in Big Papa's route!

Narrator (cont.): Once, Big Papa took my brother and me with him on his route. Neither Big Papa nor the

Cajan customers spoke good English. One store had slot machines, and Big Papa told us…

Voice of Big Papa: They just con take your money.

Narrator: But Ron was mesmerized and begged for a coin. Big Papa gave him the coin as well as his famous look of disapproval. After losing the money, he said to Ron…

Voice of Big Papa: I'm tole you.

Narrator: Ron loves to tell stories about his adventures with Big Papa. My brother cherished those times and loved to brag to Cousin Raymond that Big Papa took him fishing. One summer, Ron invited Raymond to join him on a trip to Lake Charles. Big Papa took them fishing in a sixteen-foot wooden boat. In addition to lots of fish, Big Papa caught a stingray, which he butchered savagely with a knife and hurled back into the sea. Shortly after that, Raymond had something very large on his line and begged Big Papa to help him reel it in. Everyone could see it was a baby shark, which was stupendous compared to their small boat.

Voice of Cousin Raymond: Help, help me with this!

Narrator: After watching him struggle, Big Papa asked…

Voice of Big Papa: What you con do with it when you get it in the boat?

Narrator: (*Chuckles.*) That baby shark was released into the sea where it belonged! (*Pause.*) Today, when Ron and I speak on the phone, all I have to do is mention Big Papa, and Ron comes up with an interesting or amusing story about him. It struck me one day to ask Ron to write his memories and send them to me. Here is part of what he wrote:

Voice of Ron: Big Papa had a passion for the water, and it rubbed off on me. As I grew up, he taught me how to catch crab, shrimp, and fish. While washing his boat after a fishing trip, Big Papa took off his shirt. I was amazed to see multiple scars on his chest. "How did you get those scars?" I asked. He explained that he harvested octopus, which was considered to be a delicacy by the Turks. The octopus has suction cups that adhered to his chest while he was at the bottom of the ocean. Good thing Big Papa was a barrel-chested, strong individual! I was always amazed by Big Papa's gruff voice. He once scared me just by saying hello. He was an avid plant grower, especially with gardenias. He warned…

Voice of Big Papa: Not you con play on my bush!

Voice of Ron: And we didn't.

Narrator: As for me, my fondest memory of Big Papa is going with him to see cowboy movies. During the Jim Crow era of segregation, we went to the Negro owned theater in Lake Charles, where we sat in the balcony with the white people. In my hometown of Marshall, Texas, the Negroes sat in the balcony, so I was thrilled with the novelty of role reversals. I remember riding with Big Papa in his big green Chevrolet. When he shifted, he went from first to third, never second. Aunt Maine, who lived with him, would warn…

Voice of Aunt Maine: Don't ride with Papa unless he goes to see Aunt Rosie and back to the house, never any farther than that.

Narrator: On rainy days in Lake Charles, it amazed me how the water stayed in the street and splashed the sides of the car as we rode along. It was like getting to play in the puddles with Big Papa in his car. (*Pause.*) Eventually, I contacted other family members to add to Ron's memories. Their recollections are almost as vivid and amusing as those of my brother. Most family members came from out of town to visit Big Papa and Big Mama, but Cousin Paula grew up in Lake Charles. She recalls one Saturday night when she was sixteen. Her parents were away, so she stayed with her grandparents and described the incident as follows:

Voice of Cousin Paula: My date came to pick me up there. Oh, my gosh! Big Papa rose from his chair like a giant. I introduced the boy. There was no hello, just Big Papa saying in his deep voice…

Voice of Big Papa: You better be nice to her.

Voice of Cousin Paula: My aunt wanted us to sit down and visit, but my date was white as a sheet. When I got home, I had to wake Big Papa to get back in the house. I never did that again!

Narrator: Big Papa loved his family and would visit us often in East Texas. One of my cousins wrote about the men in Marshall getting together to play dominoes. Big Papa and Grandpa Nader played dominoes in warm weather on the front porch, and at Christmas, in the middle of the living room, oblivious to all of the women and children's ruckus and jabbering. And they

SLAMMED those dominoes down. It's a wonder those dominoes survived. Her father had to learn to count in Arabic so he could call out his score in Arabic to be allowed to play with them. And Suzanne, the youngest of the cousins, recalls…

Voice of Cousin Suzanne: As I was the runt of the litter, my experiences with Big Papa center around his less active days. I would sit on the arm of his recliner and pull his ears. I couldn't believe how big his ears were, and they were a constant fascination for me. Even though I'm sure I was a huge pest to Big Papa, I don't remember him ever losing his temper with me. He seemed like a giant when he stood up; he was tall, and I was not. I can still see him getting up from his recliner and walking with his big feet! I remember vividly the day he passed away. It was a Saturday morning in 1972, and I was nine. We had recently moved to Dallas, and I was watching cartoons. Mom got a phone call, and I remember her coming to me with the news. It was impactful to me. Although we didn't have that much time together, I felt a significant loss.

Narrator: I compiled and edited these auspicious moments in an eight-page Christmas letter and sent it to my family. Sixteen of Big Mama's and Papa's nineteen grandchildren live in different parts of the U.S.; three are now deceased. The rest of us still communicate by phone and email. Lately, we've been exchanging old photos as well as childhood memories. But on the Friday before Christmas of this year, one of my cousins, Rusty Asaff, suddenly became ill and died. He was a fun-loving, gregarious individual whose energy was loved by all. Now, more than ever, I feel the urgency of connecting and staying in touch with those we love. Our last family reunion was at Rusty's house. Our next one will be his memorial service when it's safe to gather again.

<u>End of play.</u>

Moonlight and Magic

By

Anne V. Grob

Moonlight and Magic, under the title The Planting Moon, was a semi-finalist in *Little Black Dress Ink's Female Playwrights Onstage Project* and received a staged reading at Left Coast Books in Goleta, CA, April 2014. Undergoing revisions, the character of the father was added and the setting moved from a cemetery to a family home. The title became ***Pentimento***, produced by Summer Voices 2016.

Anne V Grob, a member of the Dramatists Guild, studied at SCR's Playwriting Conservatory. She has produced plays in NYC's Players Theatre SPFs of 2013-2020, winning best of festival for *Hemingway At The Larchmont, Once Upon A Sofa, The Bard of MacDougal Street, Alexa Takes Manhattan* and *Used Heart. Mouse Play* appeared in Ohlone College Playwrights Festival 2016*, and UNTITLED* placed as finalist in <u>Heartland Theatre 10-Minute Play Festival 2016</u>. For New Voices, productions of Anne's work include: *Variations On A Composition In Blue* (Summer, 2014), *How To Have A Kosher Christmas* (Holiday, 2014), *The Trouble With Art* (Summer 2015), *Pentimento* (Summer, 2016), *The Secret Chord* (Holiday, 2016), *Not Even The Moon* (Summer, 2017), *Some Simple Kindness* (Holiday, 2017), *The XYZ of It* (Summer, 2018), *A Cup O' Kindness* (Holiday, 2018), and *G.O.A.T., or Who is Alexa*? (Summer, 2019). Anne's plays appear in New Voices Playwrights Theatre anthologies, and *Variations On A Composition In Blue* was published in **The Best American Short Plays 2013-2014.**

CHARACTERS

Elise, an older woman, a spirit

Gina, a woman of childbearing age, Elise's daughter

> *At rise, a cemetery. It is an autumn day in late afternoon. There are leaves scattered on the ground, a bench at Stage Left, a grave at Center Stage. The ghostly image of an older woman stands at Stage Right, facing audience. She picks up a few leaves and studies them curiously. A young woman enters from a walkway, Stage Left. She carries a small bunch of wildflowers. She approaches the grave.*

Gina: Hello Mama. I'm here.

> *Elise turns toward Gina and extends her arms toward her. Gina does not see Elise but she can hear her.*

Elise: Is that you, my Gina?

Gina: I've missed you.

Elise: I know.

Gina: I dream about you, all the time.

Elise: For you it's a dream, for me, it's where I am.

Gina: In the moonlight. I know. Bury me in the moonlight you said. And now I understand.

Elise: Oh how I loved those nights we'd stay up for hours, talking and catching fireflies in the glow of the summer moon.

Gina: I cherish those memories too, Mama. In my dreams, they seem so real. You call to me, trying to say something. Last night you said you had something important to tell me, or give me.

Elise: I gave you something? Yes, yes I must have. I always like giving you things.

Gina; But then I lost it. Whatever it was that you gave me, I lost. And it saddened me.

Elise: Yes, I know. *(Beat.)* I lost something once. I can't recall now. Was it a rock, or a stone?

Gina: Once the stone fell out of your ring.

Elise: No, it was a baby. I lost a baby. And you would ask me, Mama, will we ever find the baby we lost?

Gina: I didn't understand, but you explained about the seed growing inside you, like the seeds we plant in the garden for the flowers to grow. Only sometimes, something goes wrong, and they don't grow.

> *Gina places the flowers on the grave. Elise approaches.*

Elise: Are those flowers from our garden?

Gina: Yes, Mama, the last of them, I'm afraid.

Elise: What are you afraid of?

Gina: It's just an expression, Mama. *(Beat.)* It's getting colder now and the trees are beginning to change color.

Elise: Is it autumn already?

Gina: Soon all the leaves will fall to the ground.

Elise: So these are leaves then, not notes?

Gina: What do you mean, musical notes?

> *Musical notes play as Elise tosses leaves in the air.*

Perhaps they are musical notes, the music of the messages left behind from those among the living. They are the discarded and forgotten sorrows of all the departed souls. The wilted flowers you carry, they are the broken promises.

Gina: These are fresh flowers. I just picked them today.

Elise: For me, they have already wilted and died.

Gina: I'm sorry. I didn't know. I thought you would…

Elise: Don't apologize to me. I can no longer collect apologies. They weigh too much.

Gina: I only wanted to bring you something, so that you will know I've been here.

Elise: Bring me stones. They are lighter than apologies.

Gina: Stones?

Elise: Each time you visit me, take a stone and place it on my grave. I have no use for sorrows and broken promises. Those are the concerns of the living. Stones are forever.

Gina: Yes, Mama. I will remember next time to bring stones.

Elise: How will you find me? The next time you come, a snow blanket will cover the ground.

Gina: I'll be here long before winter arrives.

Elise: You must not come so often. This is no place for you to spend your days. But I do hope you visit at wintertime. It will be lovely then.

Gina: I will, but…

Elise: I tell you what.

> *Elise crosses to Stage Left. Looking out over the audience, she gestures toward the sky.*

There's a little bird that nests in a tree nearby and sings to me every night. When winter comes, I shall summon the bird to lead you here.

Gina: Mama, birds migrate south for the winter. But you already knew that.

Elise: It was just a thought.

Gina: Daddy says I shouldn't be coming here now. He says I must wait a year, that it's too unsettling…

Elise: Your father is a wise man.

Gina: Then you agree?

Elise: I didn't say that. I just said he is a wise man.
Does he still sit low to the ground?

Gina: I don't know what you…

Elise: Remind him to take his medication. Soon he will
start to forget. But it will be up to you to take care of
him.

Gina: He keeps asking me to make Hiding Soup. But I
couldn't find it in your recipe book.

Elise: There is no recipe. My mother prepared it and
taught me. Did I never show you?

Gina: I think maybe you did. Is it made with lentils and
sausage?

Elise: Yes, and when we had only enough money for a
sausage or two, they would hide under the lentils.
That's Hiding Soup.

Gina: Seems easy enough. I think I can make it for him.

Elise: Daddy should not be eating lentils now. They are
too much a reminder of death. Mourning is shaped like
a wheel, round as a lentil. Daddy has eaten enough
lentils and has sat low to the ground long enough.

Gina: I want Daddy to come live with me. Don't you
think he shouldn't be alone?

Elise: No one is ever alone. But he must live with his
memories for a time. He must see his past life every day
before he can see his future life. For now, he is bound
to the temporal world, as are you.

Gina: That's what we're trying to figure out, how to manage each day. You know, Mama, I still can't imagine how I will live the rest of my life without you.

Elise: Don't think about it.

Gina: That's your answer? Don't think about it?

Elise: That's my answer.

Gina: I thought there would be more; something pithy and profound.

Elise: How about, take one day at a time? Is that better?

Gina: *(Laughs.)* I suppose so.

Elise: Or, there's more than one way to slice a cat.

Gina: *(Laughs again.)* Mama, it's "skin a cat".

Elise: What's that?

Gina: The expression is, "There's more than one way to skin a cat."

Elise: That's just ridiculous. Why would anyone want to skin a cat?

Gina: You are so funny. I don't remember you being so funny, Mama!

Elise: Well, it just goes to show you. What else did I always say? Help me remember, Gina.

Gina: Don't give up the ship. That was your favorite.

Elise: I remember more the sweet things you would say. Like when I'd read to you from a picture book. You would say, put the pictures on my eyes, Mama.

Gina: Wasn't I the clever one? I know, I will come here every day, and we can share our memories.

Elise: No; no, no, no, no.

Gina: Then I will come every week. Or once a month, when there's a new moon.

Elise: That is no life for you, nor a suitable hereafter for me. I must learn the ways of this world, and you must carry life forward.

Gina: Am I not obliged to mourn you in an honorable way?

Elise: Mourning is part of the cycle of life, as the seasons come and go. Visit here but once each season. Now it is autumn, the time of year when the almond tree bears its fruit. But for some, it is The Planting Moon.

Gina: The time for planting is the spring.

Elise: There are many moons that are the time for planting, depending on what you want to grow. The Mourning Moon only comes in November. Some call it the Fog or Snow Moon.

Gina: That's beautiful. How do you know that?

Elise: I'm not sure. *(She gestures with her arms.)* Soon all this will be painted white. It will be the time of year called "The Moon When Deer Shed Antlers."

Gina: I loved looking out the window at the moon on winter nights. You used to tell me the most wonderful stories about the moon and the stars and the heavens. And when I would ask you about the orbits of the planets, you'd explain it so magically.

Elise: Something about angels singing?

Gina: Pulling, the angels in the heavens were pulling the planets. That's what ancient people believed, before they knew about science and tides and gravity.

Elise: I like the ancient wisdom better. *(Beat.)* It's almost night.

Gina: I don't want to go.

> *Lights dim. Only the moon. Elise and Gina are face to face and can see each other.*

Elise: Child, you must.

Gina: But I want to tell you, the night you died, I felt it happen. Did you know that?

Elise: I came to you.

Gina: I was asleep, or so I thought.

> *Gina lies down on the grass.*

I felt my body float upward, off the bed.

> *Gina rises, up on her toes.*

I float up, up, and out the window.

Elise: On a moonbeam.

Gina: I hear music coming from the kitchen.

Glenn Miller music plays.

I go downstairs.

Elise: A stronger tide than light is the sound of music playing.

Gina: There you are, washing dishes without water, wearing white kid gloves.

Elise pantomimes putting on gloves, washing dishes.

Elise: Oh, did you remember to pack for me, my green valise?

Gina: Mother, what are you doing up so late?

Elise: Shh. You'll wake your father. Got to clean before I go.

Gina: Where are you going? *(Beat.)* Mama?

Elise: Take care of little… Oh, what will you name her, something pretty?

Gina: After you, Mama. I will name her after you.

Elise: Don't forget to turn out the lights. The moon is so bright.

Elise waves goodbye and slowly retreats.

Gina: And that's how I knew you had died. I looked at the clock. It was 4AM. Two hours later, the phone rang. It was the doctor calling from the hospital. He said,

"She's expired." I should have been there at the hospital, with you.

Elise: You couldn't come to me, so I came to you.

Gina: To say goodbye.

Elise: To say goodnight. As I must do now. The sun has set, and for me, it will rise again upon your return. Leave me now to my moon and my memories.

Gina: Sweet dreams, Mama.

Elise: Sweet dreams, daughter. Each moment was magical.

> *Elise returns to the bench and lies down. Gina approaches the grave. She reaches in her pocket, takes out a few photos.*

Gina: This is your new granddaughter, Elise. I named her after you.

> *Gina places the photos on the grave marker.*

Put the pictures on your eyes, Mama. Put the pictures on your eyes.

> *Gina kisses her fingertips and touches the grave as lights fade.*

End of play.

Operation: Earth

By

Linda Whitmore

Linda Whitmore is a playwright and screenwriter living in Southern California. She is a founding member of New Voices Playwrights Theatre & Workshop.

Her plays have been produced at STAGEStheatre, CA; Chance Theater, CA; Cabrillo Playhouse, CA; Costa Mesa Playhouse, CA; Vanguard Theatre Ensemble, CA; Garden Grove Playhouse, CA; Gallery Theatre, CA; Empire Theatre, CA; Mysterium Theater, CA; and Stage Door Repertory Theatre, CA.

CHARACTERS

Claudia, 20s-30s

Jim, 20s-30s

Scene 1.

> _A middle-class suburban L.A. home. The
> present. At rise, Claudia, wearing business
> casual work clothes, a satchel slung around her
> shoulders and carrying a purse, bursts through
> the door and slams down her car keys and purse
> on the entryway table. In full panic mode, she
> desperately searches the area for something.
> She grabs a pencil out of a cup sitting on the
> entryway table next to a telephone. She urgently
> searches a stack of magazines. Then she tears
> open her satchel and extracts a pad of paper
> and starts to sketch with frenzied motions. She
> scratches through what she's drawn, tears off
> the page, crumples it, tosses it on the floor and
> starts again. She is a woman possessed. Jim
> enters from another room._

Jim: Oh, hi. I didn't hear you come in.

> _Claudia ignores him and continues to sketch
> like a mad woman._

Something wrong?

Claudia: I just saw a UFO.

Jim: Excuse me?

Claudia: What part of that sentence didn't you understand? I. Just. Saw. A. U.F.O.

Jim: I heard you. But... where?

Claudia: On the way home from the office. I was stopped in the left-hand turn lane on Sixth facing east. At Alvarado. It was about a half a block in front of me... hovering over the sidewalk. North side of the street.

Jim: Uh. OK.

Claudia: I saw it.

Jim: And now you're...?

Claudia: I'm drawing it.

Jim: So you don't forget.

Claudia: Oh, ho ho! I'll never forget it... Nope.

Jim: What... what did it look like?

Claudia: It was... it was triangular shaped. It had two bright lights on the back.

Jim: OK. How big was it?

Claudia: Judging from the building next to it, about the size of a VW Bug.

Jim: OK. What color was it?

Claudia: It was gun-metal blue. With silver trim. It... it was metallic. The sun reflected off of it.

Jim: OK.

Claudia: It... it rose a bit and banked north, behind the building.

Jim: Did it make any noise?

Claudia: Totally silent. It was so… so surreal that I froze. It was like… like I was seeing it. But my mind told me this couldn't be happening.

Jim: How long did you watch it?

Claudia: No more than ten seconds. No, maybe five or six. Let's put it this way: In the time it would have taken me to get my phone out of my purse to record it, it would have been out of sight. You know what I did?

Jim: What?

Claudia: I said, "What is that?" Aloud. In my car. Alone.

Jim: What did you do after you saw it? After it went behind the building?

Claudia: By then, I was in the middle of the intersection after the light turned green! So I had to turn left! On the east side of that stretch of Alvarado, there's an apartment building and a Ross store. And bushy trees. As I drove north, I kept trying to see it emerge a block or two later; I was staring out the passenger side window so much, I'm lucky I didn't run over anyone.

Jim: Thank God.

Claudia turns the pad toward him.

Claudia: That's it. As close as I can get it.

Jim takes the pad.

Jim: Are you sure it wasn't… a, a drone?

Claudia: Does this look like a drone to you?!

Jim: Just a sec.

Jim walks to laptop on the coffee table in the living room. He types a bit and turns the screen toward Claudia. The audience doesn't see the screen.

Like this?

Claudia: Jim, that has two wings and is a hundred feet long… it's what the U.S. uses to blast buildings in the Middle East!

Jim types again on his laptop.

Jim: How about, like a civilian drone? Like you can buy at Best Buy.

Jim turns the screen toward Claudia.

Claudia: No propellers! No wings! Look at my drawing!

Jim: OK. OK. No need to yell. I'm just trying to help.

Claudia: You don't believe me.

Jim: I believe you… you saw… something.

Claudia: I did. A UFO.

Beat.

Jim: You told me that they film movies and TV shows in that area.

Claudia: They do.

Jim: Are you sure they weren't filming something about flying saucers?

Claudia: They film west of there. At the edge of MacArthur Park. I was looking through my windshield, Jim; not in my rearview mirror!

Jim: Could it have been… a, a, a kite?

Claudia: A metal kite the size of a VW Bug.

Jim: Someone else had to have seen it. There had to be people walking down the sidewalk or crossing the street.

Claudia: Gee, I'm sorry. I didn't notice. I was too busy watching ALIENTS INVADE MY PLANET!

Jim: OK. Calm down, Claudia.

Claudia: Oh my God.

Jim: What?

Claudia: You know what's just down the street east of there?

Jim: No idea.

Claudia: The police station!

Jim: What police station?

Claudia: Rampart Division! It's just down the street from there!

> *Claudia runs to her purse and begins to rifle through it.*

Jim: What are you doing?

Claudia: Calling 9-1-1.

> *Jim races to her.*

Jim: You can't do that!

> *He takes the phone out of her hand.*

Claudia: Why not?

Jim: Well. First, we're not in Rampart Division. We're in Burbank. Second, filing a false police report is illegal.

Claudia: A false report... do you think I'm lying?

Jim: No. I... I think you think you saw a UFO.

Claudia: A minute ago you said I saw something. Now you say you think that I THINK that I saw something. Which is it?!

Jim: So you're going to call the police to tell them you saw a UFO. What do you think they'll do? Put out an APB?

Claudia: They could assign a team of detectives!

Jim: Look, let's turn on the TV to see if anyone else saw it.

> *Jim turns on the TV. Claudia collapses on the couch, her face in her hands. Jim sits beside her.*

What's wrong?

Claudia: What if I'm the only one who saw it?

Jim: If it was as real as you say it was, hovering over a well-traveled part of Los Angeles...

Claudia: ...in broad daylight.

Jim: In broad daylight, I doubt you're the only person who saw it.

Claudia: There are only two explanations. One: I saw it. Or two: I saw something that wasn't there. And that's scarier than the UFO.

Jim: Unless the aliens are here to eat us. You know. "It's a cookbook!"

> *Claudia gives him the stink eye.*

You know. From "The Twilight Zone"?

Claudia: Frankly, I expected more of you.

Jim: I'm sorry, honey. You're an intelligent woman. I'm sure… you saw something. Tell me: What else is in that block?

Claudia: There's apartment buildings on both sides of Sixth. Maybe six or seven stories each.

Jim: Hmmmm. I have a theory.

Claudia: If it's another joke, keep it to yourself.

Jim: What if someone had his window open? Say the windows open onto the street. And opposite the window, on a wall, someone was playing a video game on their big screen, and the image reflected off the window and out onto the street?

Claudia sits up.

Claudia: I guess that's possible.

Jim: Not as sexy as a UFO. But a logical explanation.

Claudia: A… a logical explanation.

Jim: Whew. Crisis averted.

Claudia: What do you mean?

Jim: I mean... I mean no UFO. Just a reflection of a video game or a movie.

Claudia: What did you mean by "crisis averted"?

Jim: Well. Honey… you know how you get.

Claudia: No. I don't. How do I get?

Jim: Uh-oh. I mean. I mean. I didn't want you to lose your mind over this.

Claudia: Lose my mind? I saw something I can't explain. A reflection of a video game? Maybe. A UFO? Maybe.

Jim: Why don't you climb out of those clothes and I'll open a bottle of wine.

Claudia rubs her face and stands.

Claudia: Yeah. Yeah. That's a great idea.

Jim: That's my girl. Red or white?

Claudia begins to exit toward the bedroom.

Claudia: White!

Jim: I'll order some delivery. Chinese OK?

Claudia (O.S.): Sounds good.

Jim walks to a small wine rack on the floor and twists some bottles to see their labels. He extracts a bottle of white wine but reinserts it into the rack and pulls out a bottle of red. He walks to the hall to see if Claudia is out of earshot. Then he walks to a corner of the room and places an ear bud in one ear.

Jim: Yeah. It's me. You guys really blew it. Picked a great time for a cloaking device malfunction!

He listens for a moment.

I don't want excuses! She saw you... and God knows how many other people did, too! I told you to stop following her! I told you that she was no threat! She doesn't suspect a thing! Now we have to move up our plans. *(Beat.)* Don't blame me. We have no choice. Contact our operatives in Paris and Beijing. Operation: Bon Appétit Earthlings starts tomorrow.

Jim pauses and looks at the bottle of wine.

How should I know how they taste? I'll let you know tomorrow.

End of play.

Pandemic Encounter at the DMV

By

John Franceschini

Pandemic Encounter at the DMV was first produced in June, 2020 by the Harvard Street Theatre Company, Hemet, CA, as a Podcast.

John Franceschini is a playwright living in Southern California. He has been published by *Applause Theatre Books* and *New Voices Playwrights Theatre.* John's plays have been produced at: City Theatre of Independence, MO; St. Johnsbury Academy, MA; Simpson College, IA; The Theatre at Hollywood and Vine, MA; Starlite Players, FL; Vienna Theatre Company, VA; Paw Paw Village Players, MI; The Globe Theatre, TX; Spokane Radio Theatre, WA; West Coast Players, FL; Pend Orielle Playhouse Community Theatre, WA; Stage Door Productions, VA; Downers Grove North High School, IL; Wasatch Theatre Company, UT; Wells College, NY; Holton-Arms High School, MD, Madison Central High School, KY; Carroll College, MT, Bradley Playhouse, Conn; Stage Left Theatre, WA. In California at: Harvard Street Theatre Company; SkyPilot Theatre; Lonny Chapman Theatre; Found Theatre; Ohlone College; Three Roses Players; Theatre Out; Stage Door Repertory Theatre; Cabrillo Playhouse; STAGEStheatre; Mysterium Theater; and Empire Theatre.

John is a member of: Dramatist Guild of America, New Voices Playwrights Theatre and Orange County Playwrights Alliance.

<u>Characters</u>

Benny, male, 30s, low-key, nerdish personality. A bit clueless about women. He wants a girlfriend but doesn't know how to go about it.

Emily, female, 30s, a bit quirky, slightly dysfunctional with a disjointed outlook on life. She is a free-spirit who wants an idealistic, stable relationship.

> *Suggested sidewalk with a building façade, there is a sign on the wall which reads, DMV. At rise, Benny is standing in line and is reading some documents. Emily, carrying some papers, walks up behind Benny and then backs up while counting six feet. Both are wearing face-masks.*

Emily: Excuse me. How long have you been in line?

Benny: My mother told me not to talk to strangers. And mothers know best don't you think?

Emily: What?

Benny: I don't know who you are.

Emily: It's just a simple question.

Benny: If I get to know you it will help break the ice.

Emily: Do you have a wristwatch?

Benny: I can't answer that question.

Emily: Why not?

Benny: It was stolen from me during a mugging. Just thinking about it will send me back into therapy.

Emily: How do you tell time?

Benny: By the angle of the sun and the shadow it casts. Look at your shadow.

Emily looks down.

Now, superimpose the face of a clock on the ground. See where your shadow hits the clock. It's two o'clock.

Benny Points.

Emily: I mean, is this the line for the DMV or the loony-tunes farm? What the hell are you talking about?

Benny: Oh, I forgot to mention, you have to know where North is. It's in that direction. North is always twelve o'clock on the dial. Look again. It's a poor-man's sundial.

Emily: I liked it better when you didn't talk to me.

Benny: Do you have a cat or a dog?

Emily: You're prying into my personal life.

Benny: I've found that 'cat' people are more mellow. They don't expect too much from the animal and are easily satisfied with life.

Emily: Not a chance! (*Beat.*) And you, I suppose are a 'butterfly' person; dancing around the woods trying to catch a sunbeam.

Benny: Okay, I guess we're not strangers anymore. My name, is Benny.

Emily: Benny, you must really do well picking up ladies at a singles bar.

Benny: Bookstores or the library is where I usually hang out. Studious types appeal to me. (*Beat.*) What was your GPA in college?

Emily: What are you in for?

Benny: Pardon me?

Emily: You know, like serving time in prison. What crime did you commit to deserve the punishment of waiting in line at the DMV?

Benny: Oh, I get it… a metaphor. (*Beat.*) There was a mix-up with my application for a 'Real-ID' driver's license. So, here I am. (*Beat.*) And… what's your name?

Emily: This DMV stuff bugs the shit outta me. Why can't the state get its act together?

Benny: Offer it up.

Emily: What on earth does that mean!?

Benny: Think of the aggravation you're enduring as a penance for past misdeeds and 'offer it up' to the heavens. You'll get time off your sentence in the hereafter.

Emily: Benny, I rather get my hand caught in a car door than be in line at the DMV.

Benny: Wow! Talk about someone getting up on the wrong side of bed this morning. Are things going that bad for you?

Emily: I wouldn't have to be here if it weren't for my stupid boyfriend. Or should I say ex-boyfriend.

Benny: What happened?

Emily: We were sharing an apartment, you know, to see if things would work for us. It didn't so I dumped him and moved out. Know what the dickhead does?

Benny: I'm dying to know.

Emily: When my driver's license renewal came in the mail, the dickhead contacts the DMV and tells them I died.

Benny: You look very vibrant and energetic to me.

Emily: Precisely! Do you know how hard it is to convince someone on the phone that you're alive? I mean, you hear my voice, don't you!?

Benny: What do you have to do to prove it?

Emily: The government drone told me, "To make certain I bring my birth certificate". Hello! I said, "You should show me my 'death certificate' if you think I kicked the bucket."

Benny: You can't win when you're up against the system.

Emily: And to top it off, I've run out of friends' places to squat. So, I'm living in my car until I can find an affordable apartment. (*Beat.*) You know how hard it is to put on a skirt and blouse in a Mini-Cooper? Then I undress again and shower at the gym in the office building.

Benny: I heard the parking lot at Target's is really quiet after ten pm. You can park there overnight. And, you can use the 'head' at the twenty-four-hour, gas station on the corner of the lot.

Emily: I'm giving up on men. What slugs. Why can't I meet a regular guy like the kind I see in movies on the Hallmark Channel? It's always lollipops and roses. I just want to settle down with a good-looking stud with a beach house. I mean is that too much to ask for.

Benny: You know, you can tell a lot from a person's eyes. Since we're wearing face-masks, I don't have much else to go on.

Emily: Your eyes are bloodshot. That tells me you either had a helluva party last night or started boozing early this morning. (*Beat.*) Hey, you got a flask on you? I could use something with a kick to it to smooth out the edges. Know what I mean.

Benny: Sorry, no liquid sauce with me. (*Beat.*) I have allergies and when the pollen hits the winds, my eyes look like this.

Emily: Well, it was worth a try. What I'd give for a Cadillac Margarita right now. Do you see a bar close by? You could save my spot in line. After all, I figure we'll be here for a couple of hours. What do you think?

Benny: Maybe it's the light but I swear I can see a mischievous twinkle in your eyes. And if I were able to see under the mask, I bet I'd see a gregarious smile, very warm and welcoming.

Emily: Ah, that's sweet, Benny. No one has ever used that line on me. (*Beat.*) Hey! Wait a minute! Are you trying to chat me up!?

Benny: If I were a betting man, I'd wager that you have a creative flare and can be very artistic.

Emily: How did you know? I work at an ad agency in their graphic design department.

Benny: My mother says, I'm intuitive and a bit psychic.

Emily: Well, Benny, if you show me yours, I'll show you mine.

Benny: You mean right here, right now?

Emily: It'll have to be quick.

Benny: What if someone catches us?

Emily: No risk, no reward. Besides, you might enjoy it. Live on the edge, Benny.

Benny: Okay on the count of three… One… Two… Three!

Emily and Benny pull their face-masks down.

Emily: You look familiar.

Benny: You do too. You're gorgeous.

Emily: You're not half bad yourself. (*Beat.*) Have we ever met?

Benny: I remember now, I've seen you a number of times at the office-building cafeteria. But I didn't have the courage to introduce myself.

Emily: You should have said, hello. Don't be shy. (*Beat.*) Now, I'm glad you decided to 'Chat me up'. (*Beat.*) Alright, tell me about yourself. By the way, my name is Emily.

Benny: Emily, there's so much I want to know about you too. I'm certain we'll have to go to lunch to finish up.

Emily: Find a place that has a bar and it's a deal.

Benny: You know, if you're looking for a place to crash, I have a two-bedroom apartment. You can take the sofa.

Emily: Can I rent the extra bedroom?

Benny: My mother lives in it.

Emily: Are you still living with your mother?

Benny: Doesn't everyone?

Emily: My mother took off when I was a young kid. Never really knew her.

Benny: Gosh, I'm sorry to hear that.

Emily: It is what it is.

Benny: I think you'll like my mom, she's a warm person. And, if you give her a chance, she'll like you too. I'll tell her.

Emily: Okay. If she's alright with it so am I. (*Beat.*) When we finish up here let's catch lunch and a drink and then head to your place... I can unload my stuff.

Benny: I'll give you a hand. (*Beat.*) You know, we could carpool to work.

Emily: Let's not get ahead of ourselves, Benny. (*Beat.*) Oh, and, by the way, 'no hanky-panky'.

Benny: We could get to know each other. Maybe, become good friends.

Emily: Tell you what, once I've moved into my 'sofa-size apartment', I'll invite you over for popcorn and a Hallmark movie.

Benny: I'd like that. (*Beat.*) And you don't even have to tell me your address.

Emily: Just bring a bottle of Chardonnay.

Benny: It's a deal.

> *Emily and Benny move toward each other and do an elbow bump.*

End of play.

Small Change

By

Lynne Bolen

Small Change was first produced at *The Empire Theatre* in August, 2010 directed by Geoffrey Gread and starred Ana Maria Campoy and David Rusiecki.

Lynne Bolen is a playwright, director, producer, and actor. Her play, *Assumptions*, is included in Best American Short Plays 2011-2012, *Boulevard of Broken Dreams* in Best American Short Plays 2013-2014, *Baggage Game* in Best 5-Minute Plays, all published by Applause Theatre & Cinema Books. Her plays published in the New Voices Annual Anthology include *Spanish Masters, Winners, True Confessions, A Fair to Remember, Samantha Heart, P.I., Chicken Game, Backs*; and in the New Voices Holiday Plays, *Christmastime Machine, Past, Future & Christmas Present, On Target* [musical], and *Sunday News*. Lynne's plays have been produced at Askew Theatre Company, OR; Lion's Paw Theatre, MO; Niagara Univ, NY; Acadia Univ, Nova Scotia; Univ of Maryland; Univ of Rhode Island; Arizona State Univ; Univ of Northwestern, MN; Bethel College, KS; DePaul College Prep, IL; Hotchkiss School, CT; Oak Park High, CA; Drama West Productions; Stage Door Repertory Theatre; MUZEO; OC Pavilion Performing Arts Center; Chance Theater; Vanguard Theatre Ensemble; Gallery Theatre; STAGEStheatre; Cabrillo Playhouse; Empire Theatre; Mysterium Theater. Lynne has directed and produced dozens of shows. As an actor, Lynne has appeared in many stage productions, award winning films, and music videos.

<u>CHARACTERS</u>

Zoey, female, 30's

Zane, male, 30's

> *It is summer, time present, in Zoey's living room. Zoey is wearing a suit jacket, skirt, tank top, and high heels, her hair claw clipped in a tight bun. She has returned home from work and just sat down on the sofa. The doorbell rings and Zoey opens the door. Zane is wearing a jacket, shirt, tie, pants, slip on shoes with no socks, and glasses. He enters and gives Zoey a light kiss on her cheek.*

Zane: Hey, gorgeous, ready to go?

Zoey: Hi, Zane. I just walked in the door and haven't changed yet.

Zane: You look beautiful! You don't need to change.

Zoey: You think I'm okay? I really don't feel like changing.

Zane: I think you're more than okay. Don't change.

Zoey: Great! I'm too tired to change.

Zane: You're tired?

Zoey: Oh no, I don't mean I'm tired. I just don't want to change.

Zane: If you're tired, Zoey, we don't have to go.

Zoey: No, I want to go; unless you don't.

Zane: Are you sure you're not too tired to go?

Zoey: It's just been a long day. I've been up since five.

Zane: I sat through five meetings today.

Zoey: Are you sure you're not too tired to go?

Zane: Hey, why don't we just chill for a little bit.

Zoey: Good idea, Zane, no need to rush.

> *Zane removes his jacket.*

Zoey: We're totally compatible.

Zane: That Match.com really worked.

Zoey: Better than OKCupid or Hinge.

Zane: Or Bumble or eHarmony.

Zoey & Zane: Or Tinder!

Zoey: We have so much in common.

Zane: Both of our names start with "Z".

Zoey: Our profiles matched in almost every area. We don't drink or smoke.

Zane: We like <u>both</u> cats and dogs. And we're politically conservative.

Zoey: We were both raised as Southern Baptists.

Zane: Did you hear about that play being staged downtown called *Southern Baptist Sissies*?

Zoey: Since we're both Southern Baptists, we should definitely go see it.

Zane: You do know what it's about, right?

Zoey: *Southern Baptist Sissies?* Right. Well, we should support all Southern Baptists.

Zane: It makes sense for me to be Southern Baptist, being from South Carolina, but you were raised in Southern California.

Zoey: It was the closest church to home. Talk about conservative. It's a sin for Southern Baptists to drink, smoke, dance or wear makeup.

Zane: With that eye shadow and lipstick, I think you may have broken the rules a bit.

Zoey: I didn't say I agreed with the rules. I love to dance. By the way, Zane, I was wondering... How do you feel about not drinking? I mean it seems like everybody drinks.

> *Zane removes his tie.*

Zane: I think it's a personal choice.

Zoey: So it doesn't bother you if other people drink around you?

Zane: Does it bother you?

Zoey: Not at all.

Zane: Do you ever break the no drinking rule?

Zoey: Do you?

Zane: *(Jokingly.)* I don't wear makeup and dance, sinner.

Zoey: Well, I might bend the rules a tad and have a little bit of red wine sometimes... for the health benefits, you know.

Zane: A votre santé.

Zoey: Would you like to bend the rules and have a glass of wine, Zane, for your heart?

Zane: I don't drink wine, but you go right ahead, for your heart.

Zoey: Sounds good, it's been a long day.

> *Zoey kicks off her high heels.*

What can I get you?

Zane: You know, since you're having wine, maybe I'll join you and have a beer.

> *Zane kicks off his shoes.*

Zoey: Really? A beer? Sorry, I don't have any beer, but let me see what else I might have. Some sherry? I love to cook with sherry. No? Oh look, a bottle of vodka.

Zane: How about a vodka rocks.

Zoey: Vodka on the rocks. Sure.

> *Zoey pours the drinks and they clink glasses.*

Zane: A votre santé.   Zoey: To your health

Zane: Hey, Zoey, how often do you have a little wine, for your heart?

Zoey: Did you know that drinking red wine is better than not drinking it at all? A glass or two of red wine a day can help prevent cancer and blindness.

Zane: I'll bet you enjoy the sacramental wine. Just kidding!

> *Zoey removes her jacket and loosens the tank top from her skirt.*

Zoey: Actually, I haven't been to church in a while.

Zane: Yeah, me neither.

Zoey: Wow, really? You rock at the "Bible" category on Jeopardy.

Zane: I learned all that stuff when I was a kid in Sunday school. I remember coloring the burning bush with my red and orange crayons.

Zoey: Do you know there was a crayon color named flesh?

Zane: Yeah, I think it was renamed to Peach.

Zoey: Appalling. When was the last time you went to church?

Zane: Let's see now.

> *Zane removes his glasses.*

Junior High.

Zoey: My God! Why did you put "religious" on your profile?

Zane: Because 85% of Americans are religious. I wanted to increase my odds.

Zane pours himself another drink.

Zoey: But to lie about religion is... sacrilegious.

Zane: I didn't lie. Being religious is kinda like in remission now. Why did you indicate that you were a non-drinker on your profile?

Zoey: I wanted to increase my odds. And weed out the drunks.

Zane: And just how long has it been since you had a drink? A month? A year? Five years? Don't be a hypocrite.

Zoey: What about you being a non-drinker? I see you have no trouble slamming it down.

Zane: Yeah, right, Ms. "Little Bit of Red Wine". How many nights a week do you have a glass or two for your heart?

Zoey: I can see that reality is rearing its ugly head. Is any of your profile true, or are you a pathological liar?

Zane: Who did you vote for?

Zoey: What are you talking about?

Zane: How conservative are you? Who did you vote for in the last Presidential election?

Zoey: Stop it.

> *Zoey removes the claw clip and shakes out her hair.*

Zane: Is any of your profile true, or are <u>you</u> the pathological liar?

Zoey: Tonight has certainly been a reality check. I thought I knew you, but now I've learned I don't know you at all. I never realized you were so vicious.

Zane: You can dish it out but you can't take it. *(Sotto voce.)* Bitch.

Zoey: Dammit, Zane!

> *They glare at each other. Zoey takes a deep breath, then loudly exhales.*

You're right.

Zane: *(Beat.)* Seriously?

Zoey: I did load up my profile with a bunch of... little white lies. I was afraid to be just me, so I painted a picture of someone that I thought would be chosen from the sea of profiles. I don't know why I wasn't honest.

Zane: I know why I wasn't honest. I wanted to look better than I really am. That's the reason I used my photo from the past when I was younger and leaner. You were sweet to not ever tease me about it. My profile is the idealized me. If I told the truth about myself, nobody would want me.

Zoey: That's not true Zane. I want you.

Zane: You wanted what you thought I was; a Christian, conservative, non-drinking, non-smoking banker. When it's all spelled out, it sounds kind of boring, doesn't it? Zoey, you don't know the real me.

Zoey: I do know you, Zane. The labels may be different, but I know who you are inside. I know your heart.

Zane: You have my heart. *(Beat.)* Guess I'll have to start drinking red wine to keep it strong. To be honest, Zoey, I'm actually a loan processor.

> *Zoey removes her skirt, revealing short-shorts.*

Zoey: And I'm a legal assistant, not an attorney. But I'm planning to go to law school some day!

> *Zane removes his shirt, revealing a tank top.*

Zane: When were you planning to tell me the truth?

> *By now, Zoey is barefoot wearing just a tank top and shorts with her hair down and loose; and Zane is barefoot, wearing just a tank top and pants.*

Zoey: I didn't think we'd last long enough for me to have to.

Zane: Ditto. We have so much in common.

Zoey: So let's take inventory here. Do you smoke?

Zane: Not cigarettes.

> *Zane pulls a joint out of his pocket, lights it, and takes a deep drag.*

Emergency toke. Want a hit?

Zoey: Thought you'd never ask.

Zoey takes a deep drag, passes the joint to Zane, and puts her feet up on the coffee table.

Zane: Dogs?

Zane takes a hit and puts his feet up on the coffee table.

Zoey: Allergic.

Zane passes the joint to Zoey.

Zane: Cats?

Zoey take a hit and makes a cat noise.

Zoey: Meow! Love 'em.

Zane: We're totally compatible.

Zoey passes the joint to Zane.

Zoey: That Match.com really worked.

Zane and Zoey look at each other and smile.

End of play.

Yay! It's a Pandemic

By

Pattric Walker

Pattric Walker is a musician, song writer, playwright, director, actor, and artist currently living and working in Southern California. Of her plays that have been produced, she considers the world premiere of her full-length drama, *Dragons in New York* at the acclaimed Chance Theater in Anaheim Hills her highest achievement so far. In addition to plays, her book *33 Ways to Shape Up Your Slim Down*, various cartoons, poetry, articles, and editorials have appeared in popular publications over her lifetime.

Pattric's plays have been published in previous editions of *New Voices Playwrights Annual Anthology of Short Plays,* and *New Voices Holiday Plays*.

CHARACTERS

Kayla, female, mid to late 20's

Ryan, male, late 20's to early 30's

> *Ryan and Kayla's apartment. Ryan is sending texts. His gig bag is ready to go. Kayla is at the computer nearby.*

Kayla: *(With curiosity, wonder.)* Oh, my God. Can this really be true?

> *No reaction from Ryan, buried in his phone. Kayla goes to another web site.*

Kayla: *(Astonished.)* Oh, my God, if this is true... I wonder... Ryan, you should see this.

> *No reaction from Ryan, buried in his phone. Kayla goes to another site, frantically.*

Kayla: It is true. I can't believe it.

> *Ryan doesn't react to Kayla's outburst, picks up his bag, crosses to Kayla.*

Ryan: I'm off for my run, then I'm meeting the guys. I'll see you later.

> *Ryan gives Kayla a kiss, starts to exit.*

Kayla: Wait, no! You can't go!

Ryan: *(Stops.)* Did you just say I can't go? That sounds very much like an order. Would you care to rephrase it?

Kayla: Oh. Um, yes. Let's see... I would, but there's not really any other way to say it. You can't go out.

Ryan: *(Without anger, simply stated.)* I can, and I am. We'll talk about this when I get back.

> *Kayla races to the front door, blocking Ryan from leaving.*

Kayla: I'm not saying it.

Ryan: You just did, twice.

Kayla: I'm only the messenger here. We agreed. You can go out any time you want, and I can't because...

Ryan: You are agoraphobic. Please don't tell me you bought into some pitch that taking a pill, potion or pummeled organic plant root can cure you.

Kayla: Honestly? You know me better than that.

Ryan: I thought I did, but lately...

Kayla: What?

Ryan: *(Frustrated, sets down bag with a tiny hint of frustration, sits.)* One magic measure, two help you lifters, and everlasting survival food in the pantry. By the way, that new collagen cream won't work.

Kayla: How do you know?

Ryan: Logic, and observation. If it did, no woman would look over sixteen.

Kayla: That's beside the point. You need to stay here with me. It's for your own protection, and mine.

Ryan: Need to? Can't be food, there's enough packets for a family of fifteen. Let's see, protection. No bill collectors banging on the door. Oh, I know, you have a hit man coming to take me down, and...

Kayla: Do you always have to be so sarcastic?

Ryan: So give me a clue. What have I done now?

Kayla: Done? Nothing. You just can't go out.

Ryan: There it is again. It's Friday, my regular guys' night out. Nothing new there. You're healthy... Wait, are you? Honey, are you sick?

Kayla: I don't think so.

Ryan: Wouldn't you know?

Kayla: Apparently not. I'd have to be tested.

Ryan: Please don't tell me you're pregnant.

Kayla: Okay, I won't.

Ryan: You are?

Kayla: I just said I'm not. Why won't you ever listen to me?

Ryan: Why won't you ever go directly to the point? Wait. Are you trying to start an argument?

Kayla: No, we agreed. Never argue, just discuss. Are you?

Ryan: Just confirming. So, my darling, please tell me why I can't go out for my regular Friday night with the boys.

Kayla: *(Sexy, teasing.)* It's something that's going to make me very happy.

Ryan: Is it now?

Kayla: *(Physically enticing Ryan.)* Of course. It involves you. *(Feels Ryan getting excited.)* Ooh, is that a yes?

Ryan: *(Breaks away.)* Ah, ah, ah. I have a good memory, you know. I won't forget what this feels like later tonight when I get back. The anticipation will make it even better.

Kayla: We don't have to wait. *(Fully excited.)* Yay! It's a pandemic.

Ryan: *(With mock excitement.)* And you're so excited! *(Back to normal.)* Should I go out and buy cigars to hand out?

Kayla: Get serious, will you?

Ryan: I'll try, as soon as I figure out why an attack of germs has you so pumped.

Kayla: I'm not saying it. The Governor is. Nobody can go out. The entire state is on shut down, shelter in place. We can only leave for absolute essentials. Guys night out isn't exactly...

Ryan: Since when?

Kayla: Since ever.

Ryan: This is my lifeline we're talking about. I need time with the guys. *(Starts sending texts.)*

Kayla: I thought you'd be happy to spend more time with me. I want to spend more time with you.

Ryan: More, happily. Twenty-four seven? No.

Kayla: Well, don't blame me. Blame the Governor. You don't have any choice.

Ryan: *(Sending texts frantically.)* There's always a choice.

Kayla: *(A quiet explosion.)* If you don't want to be with me, why are we married?

Ryan: *(Rapidly sending texts.)* Kayla.

Kayla: Oh, goodie, we're going to role-play. *(As a little girl.)* Is daddy going to scold his little girl? Will I get a spanking?

Ryan: *(Reading texts.)* We talked about this. Before we got married. Damn.

Kayla: This? This what, Ryan?

Ryan: *(Sending texts.)* I keep feeling as if you want to argue. Please don't.

Kayla: Great. I marry the one man in the entire universe who expresses his feelings, and he won't let me share mine.

Ryan: *(Reading texts.)* Hoo-ah. Good man, George.

Kayla: Plans for tonight? Going well, are they?

Kayla grabs the phone from Ryan.

Ryan: *(A germ of anger, controlled.)* You're getting dangerously close to annoying me.

Kayla: Now you're catching on. *(Moves sexily toward Ryan, sets down phone.)* I want to annoy every tactile sensor you've got.

Ryan: You can definitely do that. Who says the honeymoon is over after a year or two?   *(Kisses Kayla passionately.)* Hold that thought for when I get back.

> *Ryan gets his phone and gig bag, starts to leave. Kayla grabs his bag from him, tosses it, farther away from the door.*

Kayla: If you're going to ignore the shutdown and take the risk, let me come, too. We're a team, right?

Ryan: That wouldn't work.

Kayla: I'm willing to try. The going out, I mean. Doesn't that count?

Ryan: You have no idea how much.

Kayla: Then why won't you let me go with? We do go out.

Ryan: Guy's night out is to relax, have fun, hold a beer. Sitting in a back booth in a dim restaurant is not the same as having a death grip on you to keep you from slithering to the floor in a bright, bawdy bar. What part don't you understand?

> *Building to an argument.*

Kayla: The part where you want to be with the guys more than with me.

Ryan: I need those guys. They're my anchor. They help me stay on course.

Kayla: I can do that. I'm not sure I want to be called your anchor, but...

Ryan: I only hang out with the guys one night a week. See, you win.

Kayla: I don't feel like I'm winning.

Ryan: Try to understand. It's not the same. Men bond differently.

> *During the following dialogue, Kayla nudges Ryan playfully at first, pushes him more and more, ending in Ryan finally exploding.*

Kayla: Try me.

Ryan: What do you want, Kayla?

Kayla: To be part of you. Being the hottie you come home to and shag into oblivion is great. It's the ignoring afterward...

Ryan: But that's what I need you to be. You're my pressure valve, my release from all the stress I have from work. I need the quiet.

Kayla: Why?

Ryan: Here it is. The guys warned me this would happen.

Kayla: The guys, the guys. You're more connected to them than you are to me.

Ryan: You're damn right I am.

Kayla nudges Ryan again.

Ryan: Stop that! This is going too far.

Kayla: Not far enough for me.

Ryan: *(Avoiding Kayla's reach.)* We're living my dream marriage. Aren't you happy?

Kayla: *(On Ryan's heels.)* Am I happy enough is the question.

Ryan: *(Stops, faces Kayla.)*   Is that a threat?

Kayla: I don't know, and that's as honest as I can be right now.

Ryan: What do you want from me?

Kayla: Why? Why are we living a dream instead of reality? Why don't we do more together?

Ryan: Because "do" doesn't include sitting in front of a computer absorbing documentaries and God knows what else you escape into all the time.

Kayla: You could have...

Ryan: Tried?   I did, in the beginning. I was suffocating. I can't live inside a machine.

Kayla: I never hid being agoraphobic from you. If you like going out so much, why did you marry me?

Ryan: Isn't it obvious? I'm here. *(Beat.)* Are the words that important? If I have to say it every hour I will. I love you.

Kayla: There has to be more. Something else.

Ryan: I've already told you why. Obviously, you weren't paying attention.

Kayla: Like you pay so much attention to what I say?

Ryan: *(Exploding.)* Stop it, Kayla, please. *(Ryan sits, somewhat deflated.)* I've become my father. I promised myself I'd never do that. Are you happy now?

Kayla: *(Relaxed, normal.)* Yes. Did your father get angry a lot?

Ryan: I loved and looked up to him so much. He became... so ugly.

Kayla: Thus, the introverted, agoraphobic girl who can't function in ambient noise. Feel better?

Ryan: *(Takes stock before responding.)* Oddly, yes. I do.

Kayla: I can take it. Whatever you need to unload. I want you to share it. The stress. With me.

Ryan: Come out of my man-cave?

Kayla: I'm a really good sponge.

Ryan: You did this on purpose.

Kayla: The shelter in place? How could you think I...

Ryan: The argument.

Kayla: It was the right time.

Ryan: You wanted to argue before? Why didn't you?

Kayla: Fear, I guess. We'd agreed never to argue.
Plus, you're a man. When you were ready to tell me,
you would. *(Beat.)* I got tired of waiting.

Ryan: I was afraid; of losing you. Now you've seen it.

Kayla: Did your father ever, um, was it, uh, domestic...

Ryan: No! No, he yelled, hit walls, broke some things,
once, I think. He never hit me or my mother. I love
you. I cherish you. I'd never hurt you.

Kayla: I know that. Even if you're not your father,
Ryan.

Ryan: What a night. You really took me by surprise.

Kayla: Opportunity. We're going to have to be
together all the time so...

Ryan: No boys' night out.

Kayla: I'm afraid not. You get to see how I live for a
while.

Ryan: Just you and me. Wow. It's a little scary.

Kayla: We can do this. Tell me. What can I do to
make you happy?

Ryan: Change into a man. I'm not sure I'll make it
without my guy time.

Kayla: We can watch games together. I know a lot
about all the sports you like. I don't think I can play
fantasy football, but...

Ryan: Okay, enough. I'll give you points for the effort.
Have I told you how much I love you?

Kayla: Showing is better.

Ryan kisses Kayla.

Ryan: You are definitely no man.

Kayla: Did you know that when there's too much stress, a man can't perform sexually as well as he can without stress? We'll have all kinds of time to experiment. A lot. See how less stress...

Ryan: My job. What's going to happen with my job? I've got to call my boss.

Ryan gets his phone. Kayla grabs it from him.

Kayla: Can't it wait? It's your guys' night out. I want to do something to make your night what you wanted, relaxed and fun. So, what kind of guy thing can we do?

Ryan: You can't. You are some sort of alien species, that cannot possibly, in any way, ever, act like a man.

Kayla: Try me.

Ryan breaks out in laughter.

Kayla: What?

Ryan: *(Still amused.)* I just ran through a typical guy's night out in my head, and... Man basics 101. You'd never pass. We play games, have contests to top each other...

Kayla: Darts! I used to play darts.

Ryan; Rhymes with, but no cigar. Do you remember the campfire scene in Blazing...

Kayla: Disgusting. We walked out and demanded our money back.

Ryan: Correction. You dragged me out. When I told George, he rented the movie and hosted a viewing party. It was hysterical. It's a guy thing.

Kayla: Okay, in some cases testosterone and estrogen don't mix. Now, in some contact sports...

Kayla kisses Ryan with much promise in it.

Ryan: I concede my defeat.

Kayla: I didn't thaw anything you like, since you were going to be out, so how about you run over to...

Ryan pulls Kayla back into his arms.

Ryan: I thought the Governor said I couldn't go out.

Kayla: Aren't you hungry?

Ryan: Not for anything from outside.

Kayla: But...

Ryan: Uh uh, uh. No arguing, ever again. Skip directly to the making up afterwards. Promise?

Kayla: I promise. Anytime, all day, all night if you want.

Ryan: *(Laughing, lots of joy.)* We may hate each other by the time this is over.

Kayla: We have all the time we need.

Ryan: Need. I need to call George to tell him I'm not coming over.

Ryan gestures for his phone. Kayla keeps it.

Kayla: Do you remember the stories I told you about? The ones my grandmother used to write me when I was a little girl?

Ryan: Kayla, please. Right now, you're adding to my stress. Give me the phone.

Kayla: I taped a couple of them, started my own YouTube channel. I've got some following, and I made a video to...

Ryan: That's great. You have a project to keep you busy. Please, give me the phone.

Kayla: Schools are shutting down, Ryan. Think about it. Kids will be watching more videos. You can help me write new material.

Ryan: Me? Write kid stories? You have to be kidding.

Kayla: You must have all kinds of stories up there. *(Teasingly pokes at different areas of Ryan's head.)* Or there. Or there. Your father was an international exporter-importer. You've been to all kinds of exotic places. *(Tapping in all kinds of areas at once.)* You must have stories up there.

> *Ryan takes hold of Kayla's hands, holds them behind her back, pulling her close to him. He lets the humor guide him.*

Ryan: Like the song says, I took the good times. Okay, I'll take the bad times. Now, may I have the phone, please?

Kayla: Not so bad. Did you hear me when I said I've got my own video? It's for my ad.

Ryan: Ad? We're selling things?

Kayla: Just one, so far. A sifter. Gadgets are selling like crazy. My grandmother had a way to keep the flour from flying all over the counter, and...

Ryan: You win. I'm lost.

Kayla: It's making us money. I found a company to make the sifter, have a patent pending, and it's selling. Like hotcakes, no pun intended. Twenty-five hundred in the first month. I don't know how long the sales will continue, so I thought the children's stories...

> *Ryan pulls back from Kayla, looks intently at her for a moment.*

Ryan: You really are marvellous, you know that? Agoraphobic and all.

Kayla: About that. I was serious, about trying to go out. If there are less people out during this shutdown, and you're with me, I thought maybe...

> *Ryan hugs Kayla excitedly, then pulls away, reacting as excited as Kayla had earlier.*

Ryan: Yay! It's a pandemic.

End of play.